イラン大統領 vs. イスラエル首相

中東の核戦争は回避できるのか

大川隆法
RYUHO OKAWA

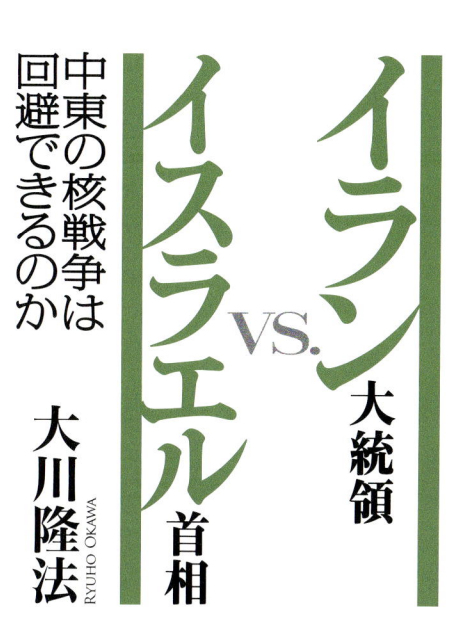

Interviews with
Guardian Spirits of
Ahmadinejad
&
Netanyahu

Iran vs. Israel
Can We Stop a Nuclear War?

イラン大統領 vs. イスラエル首相

中東の核戦争は回避できるのか

Interviews with Guardian Spirits of
Ahmadinejad & Netanyahu
— Iran vs. Israel: Can We Stop a Nuclear War? —

"Preface"

I believe that love surpasses hatred.

Mercy will save the world.

My words shall be the cornerstone of the world.

I will open the door to the peaceful future.

Because I am the Light you all have been seeking for.

I am that I am. I am the Origin of love. You all will be given hope from me.

April 24, 2012
Master Ryuho Okawa

〈まえがき〉

　私は愛は憎しみを超えると信じている。

　慈悲は世界を救うだろう。

　わが言葉が世界の礎（いしずえ）となろう。

　わが前に平和な未来が開かれるだろう。

　なぜなら私は、あなたがたすべてが探し求めてきた、その"光"なのだから。

　私はありてあるものである。私は愛の原点である。すべての者に我、希望を授（さず）けん。

2012年4月24日

人類の教師　大川隆法（おおかわりゅうほう）

Contents

Preface ... 2

Chapter One: An Interview with the Guardian Spirit of Mahmoud Ahmadinejad, President of Iran

1 Summoning the Guardian Spirits of Iran's President and Israel's Prime Minister ... 16

2 The Iran-Israel War Can Happen Any Time ... 24

3 Summoning the Guardian Spirit of Iran's President ... 32

4 Is Iran Developing Nuclear Weapons to Realize God's Justice? ... 36

5 Ahmadinejad's Guardian Spirit Demands to Know if Happy Science Is a Friend or Foe ... 44

6 Iran Will Finish Developing Nuclear Weapons in Two Years ... 50

目　次

まえがき　3

第1章　イラン大統領・アフマディネジャド氏
　　　　守護霊(しゅごれい)インタヴュー

1　イラン大統領およびイスラエル首相の
　　守護霊を呼ぶ　17

2　いつ始まってもおかしくない
　　イランとイスラエルの戦争　25

3　イラン大統領の守護霊を招霊(しょうれい)する　33

4　イランの核(かく)開発は「神の正義」の
　　実現のため？　37

5　「敵か味方か」と迫(せま)る
　　アフマディネジャド守護霊　45

6　イランの核兵器はあと2年で完成する　51

7 He Does Not Believe that the Gods of Islam
  and Judaism Are the Same   54

8 The Differences in Opinion between Khamenei
  and Ahmadinejad Are Minor   64

9 Is the Democratic Movement an American Conspiracy?   72

10 Ahmadinejad's Guardian Spirit Thinks Netanyahu
   Is a Devil   80

11 We Hope Japan Will Be the Leader of the World   88

12 About Happy Science Activities in Iran   96

Chapter Two: An Interview with the Guardian Spirit of Benjamin Netanyahu, Prime Minister of Israel

1 Summoning the Guardian Spirit of the Israeli
  Prime Minister   110

2 He Is Thinking of Attacking Iran As Soon As Today   112

3 Has the U.S. Navy Fleet Agreed to Assist Israel?   116

7 「イスラム教とユダヤ教の神は同じ」という
   認識はない   55

8 ハメネイ師との意見の食い違いは
   「些細なこと」   65

9 民主化運動は「アメリカの陰謀」か   73

10 「ネタニヤフは悪魔だ」と見ている   81

11 日本には「世界のリーダー」になってほしい   89

12 イランでの幸福の科学の活動をどう見ているか   97

第2章　イスラエル首相・ネタニヤフ氏
　　　　守護霊インタヴュー

1 イスラエル首相の守護霊を招霊する   111

2 「今日にでもイランを攻撃したい」が本音   113

3 「米艦隊が支援する」との合意がなされた？   117

4 Judaism and Islam Should Be Able to Coexist
under the Supreme God 122

5 Is Yahweh Truly the Supreme God? 128

6 Is Netanyahu's Guardian Spirit St. Michael's Soul Mate? 136

7 The Reason Why Judaism Won't Spread
around the World 142

8 What Is the True Justice of God? 148

9 A Deeply Rooted Mistrust towards Islam 154

10 Japan's Role in the World 164

11 Will the Tensions Between Iran and Israel
Lead to Mankind's Final War? 172

12 The Only Solution Is to Spread Happy Science Teachings 180

13 Israel's Surprise Attack Could Start a War? 188

14 Happy Science Must Increase Its Influence
and Gain a Higher Perspective 198

4 唯一の至高神がいれば、ユダヤと
  イスラムは愛し合えるはず　　　　　　　　　123

5 ヤハウェは本当に至高神なのか　　　　　　129

6 ネタニヤフ守護霊は
  聖ミカエルのソウルメイト？　　　　　　　137

7 ユダヤ教が全世界に広がらない理由　　　　143

8 本当の「神の正義」はどこにあるのか　　　149

9 イスラム教に対する根深い不信感　　　　　155

10 日本が世界に対して果たすべき役割とは　　165

11 両国の対立は最終戦争になるのか　　　　　173

12 幸福の科学の教えを弘めるしかない　　　　181

13 戦争はイスラエルの奇襲で始まる？　　　　189

14 勢力を広げつつ、見識を高める努力を　　　199

This book is the transcription of spiritual messages given by the guardian spirits of Iranian President Ahmadinejad and Israeli Prime Minister Netanyahu.

These spiritual messages were channeled through Ryuho Okawa. However, please note that because of his high level of enlightenment, his way of receiving spiritual messages is fundamentally different from other psychic mediums who undergo trances and are completely taken over by the spirits they are channeling.

Each human soul is made up of six soul siblings, one of whom acts as the guardian spirit of the person living on earth. People living on earth are connected to their guardian spirits at the innermost subconscious level. They are a part of people's very souls, and therefore, exact reflections of their thoughts and philosophies.

However, please note that these spiritual messages are opinions of the individual spirits and may contradict the ideas or teachings of the Happy Science Group.

Moreover, these spiritual messages were given in English, but Chapter 1, Sections 1 and 2, Chapter 2, Sections 11 through 14, as well as the questions were spoken in Japanese. English translations are provided for those parts.

本書は、イラン大統領アフマディネジャド氏およびイスラエル首相ネタニヤフ氏の守護霊の霊言を収録したものである。

　「霊言現象」とは、あの世の霊存在の言葉を語り下ろす現象のことをいう。これは高度な悟りを開いた者に特有のものであり、「霊媒現象」（トランス状態になって意識を失い、霊が一方的にしゃべる現象）とは異なる。

　また、人間の魂は六人のグループからなり、あの世に残っている「魂の兄弟」の一人が守護霊を務めている。つまり、守護霊は、実は自分自身の魂の一部である。

　したがって、「守護霊の霊言」とは、いわば、本人の潜在意識にアクセスしたものであり、その内容は、その人が潜在意識で考えていること（本心）と考えてよい。

　ただ、「霊言」は、あくまでも霊人の意見であり、幸福の科学グループとしての見解と矛盾する内容を含む場合がある点、付記しておきたい。

　なお、今回、霊人の発言は英語にて行われた。本書は、それに日本語訳を付けたものである（ただし、第１章１・２節と第２章11～14節、および質問者の発言は日本語にて行われ、それに英訳を付けている）。

Chapter One:
An Interview with the Guardian Spirit of Mahmoud Ahmadinejad, President of Iran

April 17, 2012, at the Tokyo Headquarters of Happy Science
Spiritual Messages from the Guardian Spirit of Mahmoud Ahmadinejad

第1章
イラン大統領・アフマディネジャド氏 守護霊インタヴュー

2012年4月17日 幸福の科学総合本部にて
マフムード・アフマディネジャド守護霊の霊示

Mahmoud Ahmadinejad (1956 ～)

Current President of the Islamic Republic of Iran. He graduated from the Iran University of Science and Technology, served as governor of Ardabil Province, became associate professor at Iran University of Science and Technology, and served as mayor of Tehran until his election as president in 2005. He is currently in his second term. An Islamic fundamentalist, he takes a hard line against the West and has caused controversy with repeated anti-Israel and anti-American remarks.

Interviewer
Shugaku Tsuiki
Happiness Realization Party Leader

Jiro Ayaori
Chief Editor, *The Liberty*

Translator
Yasunori Matsumoto
Director General of the International Education and Training Division, Happy Science

※ Position titles are at the time of interview.

マフムード・アフマディネジャド（1956～）
イラン・イスラム共和国大統領。科学産業大学卒業後、アルダビル州知事、科学産業大学助教授、テヘラン市長を経て、2005年、大統領に就任。現在2期目。イスラム原理主義者であり、欧米に対して強硬路線を主張。国際社会で、反イスラエル、反アメリカ発言を繰り返し、しばしば物議を醸している。

質問者
立木秀学（幸福実現党党首）

綾織次郎（「ザ・リバティ」編集長）

通訳
松本泰典（幸福の科学国際指導研修局長）

※役職は収録当時のもの

1 Summoning the Guardian Spirits of Iran's President and Israel's Prime Minister

Okawa   Today I would like to record spiritual messages related to Iran and Israel.

Japanese people may find it difficult to talk about the Middle East issues or feel it as a distant place. I think the bottom line is that they don't have enough access to information about the Middle East so they don't know enough to be able to talk about it.

Seminars are being held in Iran and three of our staffs are there now (at the time of the recording). My plan today is to call the guardian spirits of the Iranian President, Mr. Mahmoud Ahmadinejad, and the Israeli Prime Minister, Mr. Benjamin Netanyahu.

Iran's President, Mr. Ahmadinejad, studied sciences and earned his Masters at one of Iran's top schools.

第1章　イラン大統領・アフマディネジャド氏守護霊インタヴュー

1 イラン大統領およびイスラエル首相の守護霊を呼ぶ

大川隆法　今日はイランとイスラエルに関する霊言を収録したいと考えています。

　中東の問題は、日本人にとって、やや苦手というか、感覚的に遠く感じられ、難しいものかもしれません。中東についての教養があまりなく、十分に話すだけの材料がないのが現実だろうと思います。

　今、イランでセミナーが開催されており、当会の職員が三人ほど現地に行っているようですけれども（収録当時）、今日は、イランの大統領であるマフムード・アフマディネジャド氏の守護霊と、イスラエルの首相であるベンヤミン・ネタニヤフ氏の守護霊を呼んでみようと思っています。

　イランのアフマディネジャド大統領は、理系出身であり、イランの有名大学の修士課程を修了しています。知

1 An Interview with the Guardian Spirit of Mahmoud Ahmadinejad, President of Iran

He served as a provincial mayor but also received his doctorate and taught as an assistant professor at his alma mater, after which he went on to become mayor of Tehran and now President.

I imagine he received his education in English so he can speak it to some extent. Though it might sound like a regional dialect of the language, like the Kagoshima dialect in Japan, he is an intellectual and should be able to speak and understand English.

Regarding Mr. Netanyahu, he went to America during his teens, studied at the Massachusetts Institute of Technology for his Bachelor of Science degree in Architecture, and then later, he acquired a Master of Science degree from the MIT Sloan School of Management. He also studied political science at MIT and Harvard. Then he experienced working at a private company, the Boston Consulting Group, before becoming deputy chief of mission at the Israeli Embassy in the U.S., and then ambassador to the

第1章　イラン大統領・アフマディネジャド氏守護霊インタヴュー

事をしていましたが、博士課程も修了して母校の助教授になり、そのあとテヘラン市長を務め、現在、大統領になっています。

　彼は英語で教育を受けていると思われるので、ある程度、英語ができるのではないでしょうか。彼の英語は"鹿児島弁の日本語"のような英語ではないかと推定されるのですが、英語で話が通じるインテリではあるだろうと思います。

　ネタニヤフ氏のほうは、10代でアメリカに渡り、マサチューセッツ工科大学（ＭＩＴ）で建築学を学んだあと、同じくＭＩＴのスローン経営大学院の学位を取得しました。彼はハーバード大学とＭＩＴで政治学を学び、ボストン・コンサルティング・グループなど民間企業にも勤めた上で、駐米イスラエル大使館公使や国連大使となり、国会議員に当選後は、党首や首相を務めています。

1 An Interview with the Guardian Spirit of Mahmoud Ahmadinejad, President of Iran

United Nations. He entered the political arena when he was elected a member of Knesset, served as party leader, and now, Prime Minister.

Mr. Netanyahu knows American English. His English might be easier to understand than Iranian English, except that the Israeli (Yiddish) accent can be strong and sometimes difficult to understand. We'll see if the recording will be done in English or Japanese.

Iran also has a religious leader, Mr. Khamenei, who is higher in authority than the president. However, from what I read of his personal history, I don't think he can speak English at all. If we decide to record his spiritual messages then it will be in a separate session.

I expect today's spiritual messages will be given in either English or Japanese. If it is possible for them to give their messages in Japanese, we'll go with that.

(To the interviewers) You have become quite brazen these days about asking your questions in

第1章　イラン大統領・アフマディネジャド氏守護霊インタヴュー

　彼に対しては、ある程度、アメリカ英語が通じるでしょうし、彼が話す英語のほうが、イラン人の英語より、たぶん分かりやすいだろうと思うのですが、ユダヤ人訛(なま)りには独特のものがあり、分かりにくいこともあるので、霊言を英語で行うか、日本語で行うか、それは分かりません。

　なお、イランには、この大統領の上に、まだ、ハメネイ師という宗教指導者も、いることはいるのですが、その人は、経歴を見るかぎり、英語を話せないのではないかと思われるので、もし収録するとしても、「番外編」にしたいと思います。

　今回の霊言は英語か日本語のどちらかになると思います。日本語が話せたら、そちらで頑張(がんば)ります。

　(質問者たちに)最近、あなたがたは横着(おうちゃく)になっていて、日本語で質問し、私のほうは英語で答えるかたちが多く

1 An Interview with the Guardian Spirit of Mahmoud Ahmadinejad, President of Iran

Japanese while I answer in English. It doesn't help the purpose of showing this recording overseas, but if we use a translator, it will take time and some of the meaning can get lost.

But if you can maintain a good rhythm with the speakers, we'll have a smooth recording. There is a possibility that the spirit will start to speak in Japanese during the course of the interview, too.

Recording the spiritual message in Japanese will mean more work for Happy Science International Division but past cases have shown that the spirit's personality and distinct characteristics of their views still come out despite it being in Japanese.

The recording of the two spirits' messages will be done separately. It would be more interesting if we could pit them against each other in a debate, but I haven't heard that Mr. Matsumoto, who is here as an interpreter, can channel spirits yet.

第1章　イラン大統領・アフマディネジャド氏守護霊インタヴュー

なってきています。それは、海外で上映するには、あまり有利なやり方ではないのですが、通訳を入れると時間が間延びして話が通じにくいので、しかたがないかなと思っています。

　途中(とちゅう)で、向こうが英語ではなく日本語で話せるようになることもありうると思うので、間(ま)の取り方さえうまくいけば、スムーズに行けるかもしれません。

　日本語で収録すると、当会の国際局にとっては翻訳(ほんやく)の仕事が増えることになると思いますが、外国人の霊言を日本語で行っても、今までの例から見て、性格など、その霊の考え方の特徴的(とくちょう)なものは出てくるはずです。

　今日は両者の霊言を個別に行います。本当は、イラン大統領の守護霊とイスラエル首相の守護霊にディベートをさせるのが、いちばん面白(おもしろ)いのですが、通訳の松本氏について、「霊言ができる」という報告はまだ聴(き)いていないので、彼にはこの二人の守護霊は入らないと思われます。

We could experiment with the other channelers who have some command of English later on. If that arrangement doesn't work, we could also try to put one spirit in me and the other in another channeler. Since the other channeler might have difficulty, we can switch spirits in the middle.

A channeler must have a good amount of English vocabulary in order for him or her to channel messages in English.

Shall we see how it goes then?

(To the interviewers) I don't have a problem with you speaking in English, too.

2 The Iran-Israel War Can Happen Any Time

Okawa I already have a good idea of what both the Iranian President and the Israeli Prime Minister

そこで、チャネリングができ、英語も、ある程度できる人に、二人の守護霊が入るか入らないか、あとから番外編で実験してみる手もあります。もし、それで発言の際にハンディが生じるようであれば、「私とチャネラー(霊媒)とに半分ずつ交替で入れてみて、ディベートをする」という手も、あることはあるのです。

ただ、チャネラー自身に、ある程度、英語の語彙がないと、チャネリングで英語を話すのは、かなり難しいことなのです。

とにかく行ってみて、どんな感じかを見てみましょうか。

(質問者たちに)英語で話してくれても別に構わないんですよ(笑)。

2 いつ始まってもおかしくない　　イランとイスラエルの戦争

大川隆法　イランの大統領についても、イスラエルの首相についても、その考え方は、もう、ある程度、読めて

are thinking. They are both hard-liners and I see a confrontation as inevitable.

When Prime Minister Netanyahu went to meet with U.S. President, Mr. Obama (March 5, 2012), he probably went to get the green light to commence war.

If not that, then to ascertain if the U.S. would support Israel, to which I imagine Mr. Obama responded with his usual indecisive tone. On Mr. Netanyahu's part though, he hasn't said that he will attack in the next few days or weeks, but has said that he is not going to wait more than a few years either.

Meanwhile, Iran's President, Mr. Ahmadinejad, is quite a fundamentalist and has stated that Israel must be erased from the face of the earth.

At this rate, the same situation surrounding North Korea will occur in the Middle East upon completion of Iran's nuclear development. Israel would then be

はいるのです。二人とも超タカ派で、「一戦交えることを辞さず」という雰囲気ではあります。

先般、イスラエルのネタニヤフ首相が訪米し、アメリカのオバマ大統領と会談しましたが（2012年3月5日）、戦争の許可を取りに行ったような感じでしょうか。あるいは、「アメリカはイスラエルを応援してくれるか」という相談に行ったのでしょう。

オバマ大統領のほうは、例の調子で、「まあまあ、まあまあ」と言っていたのではないかと思いますが、ネタニヤフ首相のほうは、「数日、あるいは数週間以内に攻撃するわけではないけれども、数年以上は待てない」というようなことを言っていたようです。

一方、イラン大統領のアフマディネジャド氏もかなりの原理主義者で、「イスラエルは地図上から抹消されなければならない」というようなことを言っているわけです。

そのため、今のままでイランに核開発を進められたら、それが完成した暁には、北朝鮮と同じような状態が中東でも起きることになります。イスラエルとしては、イラ

at risk of an attack, therefore, it would want to crush Iran before they finish building the technological capability to do so.

Looking back at the past Middle East wars, Israel has always struck first to crush its opponents. It will be the same this time, too.

Based on that, I expect this war will break out within the next three years.

Japan is joining the U.S. and EU in putting sanctions on Iran, and is starting to reduce its oil imports from Iran.

In response to that, Iran is threatening to use its navy to blockade the Hormuz Strait, which is the only sea route from the Persian Gulf. If that happens, oil from the Middle East cannot reach oil importers including Japan.

If Iran blocks the strait, then of course Israel, but also the U.S., England, and France will join in the

ンに核開発を成功されてしまうと、イランから攻撃を受ける可能性があるので、その技術が完成する前に、イランを叩き潰しておきたいところでしょう。

過去の中東戦争を見ると、「先制攻撃をして敵を潰してしまう」ということを、イスラエルはもう何度も行っているので、今回も必ず行うはずです。

したがって、理論的に考えれば、「3年以内に戦争が始まらないとおかしい」と私は思っています。

日本政府は、今、欧米と協調し、イラン制裁に与しているというか、それに同調して、イランからの石油の輸入を削減しています。

イランのほうは、制裁への対抗措置として、「ペルシャ湾からの出口に当たるホルムズ海峡で海上封鎖を行う」と言っています。イラン海軍が海上封鎖をすれば、ホルムズ海峡をタンカーが通れなくなるため、日本には中東から石油が入ってこなくなりますし、日本以外の国にも、もちろん入らなくなります。

イランが海上封鎖をしたならば、イスラエルは当然のこと、アメリカやイギリス、フランス等も、イラン海軍

1 An Interview with the Guardian Spirit of Mahmoud Ahmadinejad, President of Iran

strike against Iran. It is clear that war will break out.

The smell of gunpowder is getting heavy in the Middle East right now.

When asked which side justice lies on, both guardian spirits will no doubt assert their own positions. This issue the Middle East is facing is two thousand years old. It will not be easy to solve.

First, we will listen to both sides of the story. If we come to a stalemate, and if the channeler can speak English, then I am thinking about experimenting to see if we can hold a debate.

(To the interviewers) You are used to this, now. I leave it to you, two, to do it well.

Mr. Tsuiki's Japanese is not the easiest to understand.

に対して攻撃を開始するでしょう。それは、ほぼ見える図式であり、戦争が始まることを意味します。

　したがって、ここ（中東）は、今、非常にきな臭い所なのです。

　「正義は、どちらにあるか」と言われれば、両氏の守護霊が、それぞれ、自分の主張を言うのは、ほぼ確実です。これは、2000年間も解決していない問題なので、解決するのは、それほど簡単ではないのではないかと思います。

　まずは、とりあえず両方の言い分を聴いてみて、決着がつかないようなら、チャネラーの英語力次第ではありますが、そのあと、両者でディベートをする実験をしてみてもよいと思っています。

　（質問者たちに）では、うまくやってください。慣れているとは思います。

　立木さんの日本語は分かりにくいので、なかなか通じないかもしれません（笑）。

3 Summoning the Guardian Spirit of Iran's President

Okawa   Shall we begin then?

The interpreter can interpret whenever he feels it is necessary, and remain silent if he does not see a need for it. The audience may not understand some of the English, but you don't have to mind them if you think you shouldn't cut in. We don't want to interrupt the flow of the conversation.

We'll start with the president of Iran. This is my first time, too, so I don't know what to expect, but let's try our best, shall we?

I wonder what sort of person he is.

(Takes a deep breath.)

I will now summon the guardian spirit of Iranian President Mahmoud Ahmadinejad to the Tokyo Headquarters of Happy Science.

3 イラン大統領の守護霊を招霊する

大川隆法　では、始めましょうか。

　通訳の人は、適宜、判断をして、「通訳が要る」と思えば言い、「要らない」と思えば黙っていてくれて結構です。聴衆には話の内容が分からないこともあるかもしれませんが、「通訳しないほうがよい」と思う場合には、そうしたほうがよいでしょう。通訳が入ると話が続かない場合もあるのです。

　イランの大統領から行きますが、私にとっても、この人の守護霊を呼ぶのは初めてなので、どうなるでしょうか。頑張ってみます。

　どのような人でしょうね。

　（深呼吸をする）

　それでは、イラン大統領のマフムード・アフマディネジャド氏の守護霊を、幸福の科学総合本部にお呼びしたいと思います。

1 An Interview with the Guardian Spirit of Mahmoud Ahmadinejad, President of Iran

(Puts hands in prayer and closes eyes. About 35 seconds of silence.)

Ahmadinejad's Guardian Spirit* (Groans.)

(About 65 seconds of heavy breathing.)

Tsuiki   Hello.

Ahmadinejad's G.S.   Huh?

Tsuiki   Are you the guardian spirit of President Mahmoud Ahmadinejad of Iran? (Interpretations have not been noted.)

Ahmadinejad's G.S.   Yeah.

Tsuiki   This is the Tokyo Headquarters of Happy Science.

* Ahmadinejad' Guardian Spirit will be noted as Ahmadinejad's G.S. from this point on.

（合掌し、瞑目する。約35秒間の沈黙）

アフマディネジャド守護霊　うーん。うーん。うーん……。
（荒い息遣いが約65秒間続く）

立木　こんにちは。

アフマディネジャド守護霊　ん？

立木　イランのアフマディネジャド大統領の守護霊様でいらっしゃいますか。（以下、通訳の発言は省略。）

アフマディネジャド守護霊　そうだ。

立木　ここは、日本の幸福の科学総合本部です。

Ahmadinejad's G.S. Ah, alright!

Tsuiki I am Shugaku Tsuiki, the Happiness Realization Party Leader in Tokyo.

Ahmadinejad's G.S. Really? Uh, huh. Tsuiki? Tsuiki? Tsuiki? Who? Tsuiki, who?

Tsuiki I am the head of the Happiness Realization Party.

Ahmadinejad's G.S. I don't know it...

4 Is Iran Developing Nuclear Weapons to Realize God's Justice?

Tsuiki Right now, Iran is developing nuclear facilities and weapons…

第1章　イラン大統領・アフマディネジャド氏守護霊インタヴュー

アフマディネジャド守護霊　分かった。

立木　私は幸福実現党の立木秀学と申します。

アフマディネジャド守護霊　本当か。うーん。ツイキ、ツイキ、ツイキ？　誰だ？　ツイキって誰だ？

立木　幸福実現党の責任者でございます。

アフマディネジャド守護霊　知らないな。

4　イランの核開発は 「神の正義」の実現のため？

立木　今、イランは核開発を進めていますが……。

1 An Interview with the Guardian Spirit of Mahmoud Ahmadinejad, President of Iran

Ahmadinejad's G.S.   Is there a problem?

Tsuiki   It is becoming an international issue.

Ahmadinejad's G.S.   No, no, no, it's not an *international* issue. No, no! It's just a problem between two countries.

Tsuiki   Two countries?

Ahmadinejad's G.S.   Between Israel and Iran.

Tsuiki   You often mention that you want to eliminate Israel off the face of the earth.

Ahmadinejad's G.S.   Eliminate? No, no, no, not eliminate. I mean to massacre. We don't need…

Tsuiki   So, is that why you are developing nuclear

第1章　イラン大統領・アフマディネジャド氏守護霊インタヴュー

ｱﾌﾏﾃﾞｨﾈｼﾞｬﾄﾞ守護霊　何か問題があるか。

立木　それが、今、国際社会で非常に問題になっています。

ｱﾌﾏﾃﾞｨﾈｼﾞｬﾄﾞ守護霊　国際社会だって？　違う、違う。それは２国間の問題にすぎない。

立木　２国間の？

ｱﾌﾏﾃﾞｨﾈｼﾞｬﾄﾞ守護霊　そうそう。イスラエルとイランだ。

立木　あなたは、「イスラエルは地図上から抹消されなければならない」ということを繰り返し発言されています。

ｱﾌﾏﾃﾞｨﾈｼﾞｬﾄﾞ守護霊　抹消？　いやいや、抹消ではない。皆殺しだ。われわれはイスラエルを必要としていない。

立木　やはり、それを意図して、核兵器を開発されてい

1 An Interview with the Guardian Spirit of Mahmoud Ahmadinejad, President of Iran

facilities and weapons?

Ahmadinejad's G.S.   Ha, ha, ha! No, no, no.

On behalf of God, we are being asked to help God to do the right things. This means to realize justice in this world, for Him, Elohim. It's your word, Elohim.

Tsuiki   What is "justice" for Iran?

Ahmadinejad's G.S.   Just to obey the words of God.

Tsuiki   You spoke of "justice for God," but there is very little freedom in Iran.

Ahmadinejad's G.S.   No! No! No. No. No.

Tsuiki   When President Ahmadinejad was reelected

るわけですね？

アフマディネジャド守護霊　ハハハ。違う、違う。
　われわれは、神を助けるために、神の代理人として、正しいことをなすことを求められているのだ。それは、「神のために、この世に正義を実現する」という意味だ。その神とは、君たちの言うエローヒムだね。

立木　イランの「正義」とは、どういうことを意味するのでしょうか。

アフマディネジャド守護霊　神の言葉にただ従うことだ。

立木　あなたは、「神の正義」とおっしゃいますけれども、イラン国内では、「自由」が非常に制限されています。

アフマディネジャド守護霊　いやいや。違う、違う。

立木　３年前、あなたは大統領に再選されましたが、そ

1 An Interview with the Guardian Spirit of Mahmoud Ahmadinejad, President of Iran

three years ago, people claimed that the election was fraudulent and held protests against the election results.

Ahmadinejad's G.S.   You are a very minor person. You need to have some sort of title in Japan, such as "President," "Prime Minister," or "Minister." At the least, you need to be a minister of Japan.

Tsuiki   I hope to become the Prime Minister in the future.

Ahmadinejad's G.S.   Huh? In the 22nd century, maybe?

Tsuiki   (Smiles wryly.) I hope to become the Prime Minister sooner.

第1章　イラン大統領・アフマディネジャド氏守護霊インタヴュー

のとき、「選挙に不正があったのではないか」ということで、抗議運動が起きました。

アフマディネジャド守護霊　君はとても小さな人物だ。君は、日本の総理大臣とか、何か肩書を持つべきだ。首相か、最低でも大臣だな。

立木　将来的にはそれを考えております。

アフマディネジャド守護霊　22世紀かな？

立木　（苦笑）いやいや。もう少し近い将来です。

5 Ahmadinejad's Guardian Spirit Demands to Know if Happy Science Is a Friend or Foe

Ahmadinejad's G.S. (Pounds on the table with his fist.) Are you a friend of our country, or not? It's very important to us.

Tsuiki Japan imports crude oil from Iran, so I think that Japan's relationship with Iran is very important. However…

Ahmadinejad's G.S. You are a materialist, right?

Tsuiki No. I believe in a religion.

Ahmadinejad's G.S. You only need crude oil?

Tsuiki No. This is a far more complicated issue than

5 「敵か味方か」と迫る
　　アフマディネジャド守護霊

アフマディネジャド守護霊　君は、わが国の友人か、それとも敵か！（机を叩く）　そこが、われわれにとって重要だ。

立木　イランからは原油を輸入しておりますので、日本とイランは大事な関係にあると思っております。ただ……。

アフマディネジャド守護霊　君は唯物論者か。そうだろう？

立木　いいえ。私は宗教を信じております。

アフマディネジャド守護霊　欲しいのは原油だけか。

立木　いえいえ。ただ、ここは、非常に難しい問題をは

just importing crude oil. Like Iran, America is also seeking God's justice…

Ahmadinejad's G.S. No, no, no, no, they are seeking only money.

Tsuiki That's not necessarily true. I understand that both sides have their reasons.

Ahmadinejad's G.S. No, no, no, no.
That attitude is very, very confusing. And people will be in great dismay if you take that kind of stance. It's not good.
You must decide! Just one side! God's side or the devil's side? Which one?

Tsuiki We heard that Iran is collaborating with North Korea on its development of nuclear weapons and missile technology.

らんでいると思います。アメリカはアメリカで、「神の正義を追求している」と考えているでしょうし……。

アフマディネジャド守護霊　いやいや。アメリカが求めているのは金(かね)だけだ。

立木　必ずしも、そうではないと思います。私としては、「両者それぞれに正当性がある」と認識しています。

アフマディネジャド守護霊　いやいや。違(ちが)う。
　その態度は、そうとうな混乱をつくる。もし、そういう姿勢を取るなら、人々は大いに落胆(らくたん)するだろう。それは、よいことではない。
　君は、神の側に立つのか、悪魔(あくま)の側に立つのか、それを決めなければならない。どちらだ？

立木　「イランは、北朝鮮(きたちょうせん)の核(かく)開発やミサイル開発に協力している」という情報も得ているのですが……。

1 An Interview with the Guardian Spirit of Mahmoud Ahmadinejad, President of Iran

Ahmadinejad's G.S. Are there any problems with that?

Tsuiki   Yes. That is something Japan cannot allow.

Ahmadinejad's G.S.   No! You should prepare for them, yourself. You should make your own self-defense system. It's a good chance for you.

Tsuiki   I understand your perspective. However…

Ahmadinejad's G.S.   Change! "Change" should be your party's policy. It should be your party's new policy. For instance, "Change Japan! Defend Japan!" That is the attitude of the Iranian people.

Tsuiki   I don't think it is right for you to support an enemy of Japan.

Ahmadinejad's G.S.   Government. Right?!

アフマディネジャド守護霊　それに何か問題があるのか。

立木　ここは、日本にとって見過ごせないところです。

アフマディネジャド守護霊　違う。君たちは自分たちで準備すべきだ。自主防衛の手段を持つべきだ。今がチャンスだぞ。

立木　そういう見方もありますが、ただ……。

アフマディネジャド守護霊　変革だ！　変革は、君たちの政党の方針だろう？　君たちの政党の新しい方針にすべきだ。「日本を変えよう。日本を敵から守ろう」と。それはイラン国民の姿勢でもある。

立木　ただ、日本の敵を支援(しえん)するのは、よくないのではないでしょうか。

アフマディネジャド守護霊　それは政府のほうだ。そうだろう？

6 Iran Will Finish Developing Nuclear Weapons in Two Years

Ayaori May I change the subject? I would like to ask about the issues in the Middle East.

Iran's nuclear program seems to be progressing steadily. When do you think the nuclear weapons will be ready to use?

Ahmadinejad's G.S. Two years.

Ayaori I understand that Israel wants to take military action and attack Iran's nuclear facilities. How do you intend to react to that?

Ahmadinejad's G.S. They are disciples of the devil, so they are evil people. They should be "evaporated" from the earth!

6 イランの核兵器はあと2年で完成する

綾織　日本の問題は少し置いておきまして、中東の問題について、お伺いしたいと思います。
　イランの核開発はかなり進んでいると思いますが、あと、どのくらいで完成する見通しでしょうか。

アフマディネジャド守護霊　2年だ。

綾織　イスラエルは、「軍事行動を起こして、イランの核施設を破壊したい」と思っているわけですが、イランとしては、これに対して、どう対応するおつもりですか。

アフマディネジャド守護霊　彼らは悪魔の弟子だから、悪人だ。彼らは、地上から"蒸発"するべきだ！

1 An Interview with the Guardian Spirit of Mahmoud Ahmadinejad, President of Iran

Ayaori Will you be using nuclear weapons, or do you plan to retaliate sooner using other weapons?

Ahmadinejad's G.S. It's a top secret.

Ayaori I see.

Ahmadinejad's G.S. Our top secret.

But we are the owner of our Middle East area. Do you understand what I mean? The Middle East belongs to us. Do you understand?

The Iranian people is the real leader, nowadays. So we must adopt the "typical" attitude, toward them. We really must. Since we are the leaders, we must decide and act.

Ayaori If Israel is able to convince the United States, the United States may choose to take military action. What is your opinion of President Obama?

第1章　イラン大統領・アフマディネジャド氏守護霊インタヴュー

綾織　それは、「核を使う」ということでしょうか。あるいは、それ以前に、「何か反撃をする」ということですか。

アフマディネジャド守護霊　それは最高機密だ。

綾織　おお。

アフマディネジャド守護霊　最高機密だ。
　われわれは中東地域の持ち主だ。分かるか。中東は、われわれに属している。それを理解しているのか。

　イラン人は、現在、中東における真の指導者なのだ。だから、われわれは、イスラエルに対して、中東を代表する態度を取らなければならない。われわれは指導者だから、決意し、事をなすべきなのだ。

綾織　イスラエルに説得されて、アメリカが軍事行動を起こす可能性もあるわけですが、オバマ大統領については、どのように見ておられますか。

Ahmadinejad's G.S. Obama… umm. He has a weak heart in him. He's very weak and indecisive. He is indecisive.

Ayaori So you do not think President Obama will take action.

Ahmadinejad's G.S. Since he is indecisive, he cannot make such a big decision. That's what I guess.

7 He Does Not Believe that the Gods of Islam and Judaism Are the Same

Ayaori If nothing changes, it seems that war is inevitable. Do you think there is a peaceful solution to the conflict between Iran and Israel?

アフマディネジャド守護霊　オバマか……。うーん。彼は心の弱さを持っている。非常に弱くて、決断ができない。彼は優柔不断だ。
　　　　　　　　ゆうじゅう ふ だん

綾織　実際には軍事行動を起こさないだろうと見ておられるわけですね？

アフマディネジャド守護霊　彼は優柔不断だから、大きな決断はできないと私は思う。

7　「イスラム教とユダヤ教の神は同じ」という認識はない

綾織　このままでは、イスラエルとの戦争は避けられそうにありませんが、和解の道を見いだすことは難しいのでしょうか。

1 An Interview with the Guardian Spirit of Mahmoud Ahmadinejad, President of Iran

Ahmadinejad's G.S.   Yes, you can expect some way of reconciliation.

One way is to exile them from our land to America or other countries. That is one way.

And the next way is to make them all perish. This is the second way.

And the third way is for us, the Iranian people, to let ourselves be massacred.

These three ways are waiting for us.

Tsuiki   Religion will be a very big issue in reconciling the two countries.

Ahmadinejad's G.S.   God is with us!

Tsuiki   What would you do if you learned that the Gods of Islam and Judaism are the same? [Note]
p.62

Ahmadinejad's G.S.   If that God is our true God,

第1章　イラン大統領・アフマディネジャド氏守護霊インタヴュー

アフマディネジャド守護霊　そう。君たちは、彼らと和解する方法を期待していい。

　一つ目は、彼らが、われわれの土地から出て、アメリカや他の国に亡命すること。これが第一の方法だ。

　二つ目は、彼らを全滅(ぜんめつ)させること。これが第二の方法だ。

　三つ目は、われわれイラン国民が、われわれ自身を虐殺(ぎゃくさつ)すること。

　これらの三つの方法が、われわれを待ち受けている。

立木　和解のためには、宗教的な問題が非常に大きいと思うのですが。

アフマディネジャド守護霊　神は、われわれと共にある。

立木　もし、「イスラム教の神とユダヤ教の神は、同じ神である」[注]ということが判明した場合、どうされますか。
p.63

アフマディネジャド守護霊　もし、その神が本物の神であるなら

57

1 An Interview with the Guardian Spirit of Mahmoud Ahmadinejad, President of Iran

He must, or He will, declare that this is our land. He must say so. If He doesn't say that, then He is a devil.

Ayaori You mentioned the name Elohim earlier. Do you believe Him to be God?

Ahmadinejad's G.S. No, I believe in Allah. It was just my paying lip service to you.

Ayaori We believe that both Allah and Elohim are the same being. Is it possible for you to believe this?

Ahmadinejad's G.S. It's difficult, very difficult.

Ayaori You are the guardian spirit of President Ahmadinejad. Who do you normally speak with in the spirit world of Islam?

ば、神は、「ここは、おまえたちの土地である」と宣言するだろう。あるいは、そう宣言しなければならない。神ならば、そう言うはずだ。もし、そう言わないならば、それは悪魔だ。

綾織　先ほど、エローヒムという名前も出ましたが、あなたが信じている神は、エローヒムなのでしょうか。

アフマディネジャド守護霊　いいや、アッラーだ。さっきのは、君たちへのリップサービスだよ。

綾織　私たちからすれば、同じ存在ということになるのですが、そういう認識には至らないのでしょうか。

アフマディネジャド守護霊　それは難しい。非常に難しい。

綾織　あなたは守護霊であるわけですが、イスラム教の霊界において、普段、どのような指導者たちと話をされていますか。

1 An Interview with the Guardian Spirit of Mahmoud Ahmadinejad, President of Iran

Ahmadinejad's G.S. You, Japanese people, don't know about great figures in Iranian history. So it will only sound like nonsense. It doesn't make sense to tell you.

Ayaori Are there any spirits whom the Japanese people would recognize?

Ahmadinejad's G.S. On the other hand, if you ask the Iranian people about famous Japanese historical figures, we also don't know much about them.

Tsuiki In his spiritual messages, Muhammad said that he is strongly promoting Iran's nuclear program. Does Muhammad give direct guidance to President Ahmadinejad?

第1章　イラン大統領・アフマディネジャド氏守護霊インタヴュー

アフマディネジャド守護霊　君たち日本人は、イランの歴史上の偉大な人物を知らないだろう。だから、その問いには意味がない。意味をなさないのだよ。

綾織　日本人にも分かるような方はいらっしゃらないのですか。

アフマディネジャド守護霊　反対に、もし、君がイランの人々に、日本の有名な歴史上の人物について訊いたとしても、誰も知らないだろう。

立木　以前、霊言のなかで、ムハンマド様が、「私はイランの核開発を強力に推進している」とおっしゃっていましたが（『世界紛争の真実』〔幸福の科学出版刊〕第1章参照）、ムハンマド様から大統領に、直接、霊的な指導が及んでいるのでしょうか。

1 An Interview with the Guardian Spirit of Mahmoud Ahmadinejad, President of Iran

Ahmadinejad's G.S.   That is Muhammad! I'm sure! Very sure.

> Note: Allah, the one and only God in Islam, is not a proper noun but is simply the Arabic word for "God" or "Creator." In Middle Eastern religions, Elohim is recognized as the Creator (Elohim is another name of El Cantare). Yahweh and Elohim are both gods that appear in the Old Testament, the Jewish scripture. This means that Elohim guided both Islam and Judaism. Refer to *The Golden Laws* (Lantern Books).

第1章　イラン大統領・アフマディネジャド氏守護霊インタヴュー

アフマディネジャド守護霊　それはムハンマドだ。確かに、間違いない。

　　［注］イスラム教における唯一神・アッラーとは、固有名詞ではなく、創造主を意味する「神」のことであり、中東の信仰において創造神を特定するならば、「エローヒム」（エル・カンターレの別名）になる。一方、ユダヤ教の聖典である『旧約聖書』には、ヤハウェのほかに、「エローヒム」という神も出てくる。つまり、エローヒムは、イスラム教もユダヤ教も指導していたのである。『黄金の法』（幸福の科学出版刊）参照。

8 The Differences in Opinion between Khamenei and Ahmadinejad Are Minor

Tsuiki   Since Iran is an Islamic republic (a republic based on Islamic teachings), Supreme Leader Khamenei has more power than the president. Does President Ahmadinejad agree with the opinions of Supreme Leader Khamenei?

Ahmadinejad's G.S.   Hmm…almost. Almost.

Tsuiki   The president fought with Supreme Leader Khamenei about cabinet appointments and there seems to be tension between the two. In the parliamentary election this March, the Supreme Leader Khamenei faction won against the President Ahmadinejad faction in a landslide. Moreover, the president was even summoned before parliament to

8 ハメネイ師との意見の食い違いは「些細なこと」

立木　イランは、イスラム共和制（イスラムの教えに基づいた共和制）ということで、大統領の上に、ハメネイ師という最高指導者がいらっしゃるわけですが、その方とは、考えが一致しているのでしょうか。

アフマディネジャド守護霊　うーん、ほぼ。だいたいね。

立木　閣僚の人事をめぐって、不仲が取り沙汰されていますし、今年３月の議会選挙では、ハネメイ師支持派が圧勝して大統領派は負けました。また、「経済政策をめぐって、大統領が国会で喚問を受ける」ということも起きています。

answer questions over alleged mismanagement.

Ahmadinejad's G.S. You are not a politician. You are a journalist.

Tsuiki I hope to be a politician who has journalistic curiosity.

Ahmadinejad's G.S. I think that it's a minor point.

Iran is a very difficult country. You don't understand, exactly, the system of our politics. One part of it consists of a religious policy, and on the other side, there is a policy that is practical, political, and economic. These two sometimes collide though, so the reality that occurs can become very confusing.

He is the Supreme Leader of the Iranian people. But, he doesn't have enough knowledge about real economics, politics, foreign trade, and etc. Since I'm more intelligent, smart, and pragmatic, compared to

第1章　イラン大統領・アフマディネジャド氏守護霊インタヴュー

アフマディネジャド守護霊　君は政治家ではない。ジャーナリストだな。

立木　私は、そういう面も持ちながら、政治活動をしようと思っております。

アフマディネジャド守護霊　些細なことだと思う。
　イランは、非常に難しい国だ。君たちは、イランの正確な政治システムを理解していない。一つには「宗教的な方針」があり、もう一つには「現実的な政治・経済の政策」がある。この二つが、ときおり互いに衝突するため、現実は非常に複雑だ。

　彼（ハネメイ師）は、われわれイラン国民にとって至高の存在である。しかし、彼は、現実の経済や政治、海外との貿易といったことについて十分な知識を持っていない。私のほうが、むしろ、彼より知的で頭がよく、実

1 An Interview with the Guardian Spirit of Mahmoud Ahmadinejad, President of Iran

him, there are chasms between us and our opinions sometimes differ.

But it's not such a big problem, I think. The only important conclusion is about the glory of God. How to make our country prosper.

Tsuiki   A few decades have passed since the Iranian Revolution, but it seems Iran has made very little economic progress.

Ahmadinejad's G.S.   You, you, you, behave yourself. Please check and control your words carefully! I am the president of …

Tsuiki   Pardon me, but I must say that economically, Iran is far behind America and the European countries.

Ahmadinejad's G.S.   (Pounds on the table three

用主義なのだ。そのため、ときどき、われわれの意見は食い違う。

　しかし、それは、そんなに大きな問題ではないと思う。唯一の結論は、神の栄光だ。「われわれの国をいかに繁栄させるか」ということが大事なのだ。

立木　しかし、イラン革命が起きてから、すでに数十年たちますが、イランには、まだまだ経済的に発展していない面があるのではないでしょうか。

アフマディネジャド守護霊　君、君！　慎みなさい！　自分の言葉をよく確認し、統御しなさい！　私は大統領なんだぞ！

立木　すみません。失礼しました。ただ、欧米に追いつくところまでは、まだ行っておられないように見えるのですが。

アフマディネジャド守護霊　（机を3回叩く）無礼だ！　君は銃で

1 An Interview with the Guardian Spirit of Mahmoud Ahmadinejad, President of Iran

times.) Rude! (Pretends to fire a gun.) You must... "bang!" You should die in Iran.

Tsuiki   Iran had allowed Japan to develop Iran's oil fields...

Ahmadinejad's G.S.   You are a materialist! I don't like such kinds of people.

Tsuiki   So I do not have such a negative image of Iran. I believe that Iran is a very important region, and Japan would like to extend any support we can to help Iran's economy to develop towards a more ideal state.

Ahmadinejad's G.S.   You should abandon your goal to become a politician. You should work for a small newspaper company or some other place like that. You are a writer. Just a writer.

撃たれるに違いない(銃で撃つしぐさをする)。君はイランで死ぬべきだ。

立木　日本としては、イランに油田開発などで便宜を図っていただいたこともあるので……。

アフマディネジャド守護霊　君は唯物論者だ!　私は、そのような人間は嫌いだ。

立木　私自身には、イランに対する悪いイメージはなく、非常に大事な地域だと思っていますし、イラン経済を何とか理想的な状態に持っていくためにも、日本が協力できることはさせていただきたいと思っております。

アフマディネジャド守護霊　政治家になるのはあきらめたまえ。君は、小さな新聞社とか、そういうところで働くべきだ。君は記者だ。ただの記者ではないのか。

1 An Interview with the Guardian Spirit of Mahmoud Ahmadinejad, President of Iran

(Pointing to Ayaori.) He's a writer also. I know.

Ayaori   Well, I…

Ahmadinejad's G.S.   Oh, you can be a politician? Ok, ok, great. Better.

Ayaori   I am not a politician, but my work is related to journalism.

9 Is the Democratic Movement an American Conspiracy?

Ayaori   So, currently the relationship between Iran and Israel is an important issue. However, since last year, the Arab Spring democratic movement has been spreading through the Islamic countries.

What do you think of this movement? I suppose you could view this as a movement to liberate

彼(綾織)も記者なのか。私には分かるよ。

綾織　まあ、私のほうが……。

アフマディネジャド守護霊　君(綾織)は政治家になれるのか。分かった。いいだろう。少しはましだろう。

綾織　いや、違います。私のほうが、ジャーナリズムの仕事に近いのですけれども。

9　民主化運動は「アメリカの陰謀」か

綾織　ところで、今、イランとイスラエルの関係が大きな争点になっているわけですが、イスラム圏全体を見ると、去年から、「アラブの春」という民主化運動が大きな動きになっています。
　これについては、どのように見ておられますか。「アメリカが支援する独裁者からの解放」という見方もできる

1 An Interview with the Guardian Spirit of Mahmoud Ahmadinejad, President of Iran

countries from dictators under U. S. control.

Ahmadinejad's G.S. There could be some kind of conspiracy behind it. The CIA or another kind of evil political machine is probably working for that. Jewish groups from the United States of America might be receiving black money for it.

Ayaori Do you think that the Arab Spring will affect Iran?

Ahmadinejad's G.S. Mm, hmm. I guess so.

Ayaori Are you trying to suppress the movement in Iran right now?

Ahmadinejad's G.S. You are not such a good person, either.

とは思いますが。

アフマディネジャド守護霊　何か陰謀のようなものがあるはずだ。つまり、ＣＩＡやそういう類の邪悪な政治組織が画策しているのだ。アメリカのユダヤ人グループからブラックマネー（闇資金）をもらっているはずだ。

綾織　ということは、「イラン国内にも、その影響が及んでくるかもしれない」と？

アフマディネジャド守護霊　おそらくそうだろう。

綾織　今は、それを押さえつけている状態ですか。

アフマディネジャド守護霊　君も善人ではないな。

1 An Interview with the Guardian Spirit of Mahmoud Ahmadinejad, President of Iran

Ayaori It seems like you are struggling to keep the movement out of Iran.

Ahmadinejad's G.S. It's very difficult! We're in a very difficult situation. We need power! We need concentration! We need to gather our power, all the national power we have, to resist against the evil intentions of Israel.

So, you just said that we have suppressed our nation, our people. That's what you said. But that is only one side. You are looking at it from only one angle, like a journalist from America or Europe.

But, we are just preparing for the next big collision with that bad and powerful country.

Are you summoning Netanyahu (his guardian spirit) next?! He doesn't like justice. And he asked the United States and other European countries (for support). That's not something we can tolerate.

第1章　イラン大統領・アフマディネジャド氏守護霊インタヴュー

綾織　ご苦労されているのかなと思いまして。

アフマディネジャド守護霊　非常に難しい状況にある。われわれには力が必要だ。集中が必要だ。イスラエルの邪悪な意図に抵抗するために、われわれの力を、国民全体の力を結集しなければならない。

　君は、われわれが国民を抑圧していると言ったが、それは一面にしかすぎない。一つの角度だけから見て、君は、アメリカやヨーロッパのジャーナリストのように考えるのだろう。
　しかし、われわれは、悪の大国との次なる大きな衝突のために、準備をしているだけなのだ。
　私の次は、ネタニヤフ（守護霊）を呼ぶのか。彼は正義を嫌う。彼はアメリカ合衆国やヨーロッパ諸国に（支援を）求めたが、それは、われわれの我慢の限度を超えている。

1 An Interview with the Guardian Spirit of Mahmoud Ahmadinejad, President of Iran

Ayaori   The Arab Spring…

Ahmadinejad's G.S.   Conspiracy!!

(Pounding on the table.) (In Japanese.) *Inbo da, inbo. Wakaruka?* (It's a conspiracy! A conspiracy, I tell you!! Do you understand?!)

Ayaori   We were told that the Arab Spring was being guided by Allah, or Elohim. (Note: Muhammad spoke about this in his spiritual messages, "What is Happening in the Middle East?" recorded on August 23, 2011.)

So by trying to suppress this democratic movement, you are actually defying the will of Allah.

Ahmadinejad's G.S.   That's just about a Japanese god. The Japanese god needs oil. That's the main point.

Ayaori   Elohim is also the God of the Middle East.

第1章　イラン大統領・アフマディネジャド氏守護霊インタヴュー

綾織　「アラブの春」は……。

アフマディネジャド守護霊　陰謀だ！
　（机を叩きながら）陰謀だ、陰謀。分かるか。

綾織　「中東での民主化運動は、アッラー、つまりエローヒムが天上界から指導している」と聞いております。（注。2011年8月23日「中東で何が起こっているのか（ムハンマドの霊言）」を収録した際、ムハンマドの霊はそのように語っていた。）
　そうすると、民主化運動を抑えるのは、アッラーの神に反抗するかたちになってしまうと思います。

アフマディネジャド守護霊　それは"日本の神"だ。"日本の神"が石油を求めているのだ。それが主要なポイントだ。

綾織　いえいえ。エローヒムは中東の神です。

Ahmadinejad's G.S. No, no, no, no. There's a Japanese Elohim.

Ayaori No. Elohim is the God of the Middle East. You are actually revolting against your God, Allah.

Elohim is the same being as Allah.

Ahmadinejad's G.S. Allah, Allah. We love Allah. We are one!

10 Ahmadinejad's Guardian Spirit Thinks Netanyahu Is a Devil

Tsuiki I think that economic prosperity is a part of God's glory, but the Islamic countries have prospered very little.

Perhaps you are not truly governing Iran in

ｱﾌﾏﾃﾞｨﾈｼﾞｬﾄﾞ守護霊　違う、違う。日本の"エローヒム"だ。

綾織　いいえ、違います。エローヒムは、中東にいらっしゃいます。つまり、あなたは、アッラーに反対するような立場に立つことになってしまうわけです。
　エローヒムとは、結局、アッラーですよね？

ｱﾌﾏﾃﾞｨﾈｼﾞｬﾄﾞ守護霊　アッラー、アッラー。われわれはアッラーを愛している。われわれは一体だ。

10　「ネタニヤフは悪魔だ」と見ている

立木　神の栄光があるのであれば、やはり、それは経済的な繁栄を伴うと思うのですが、イスラム教国は、そこがいまひとつ物足りません。
　忖度するに、神の御心から少しずれている部分がある

1 An Interview with the Guardian Spirit of Mahmoud Ahmadinejad, President of Iran

accordance to God's will. What do you think about that?

Ahmadinejad's G.S.   We are seeking justice.

Tsuiki   So you are seeking justice, but Iran has not prospered.

I am hoping that Japan could help reconcile the Islamic countries in the Middle East and the western countries.

I heard that former Prime Minister Hatoyama was loitering about in Iran recently.

Ahmadinejad's G.S.   Ah, Mr. Hatoyama is a better and much kinder person than you two.

Tsuiki   (Smiles wryly.) Well Mr. Hatoyama's reputation and popularity has plummeted in Japan.

のではないかと思うのですが、そのあたりについてはいかがでしょうか。

アフマディネジャド守護霊　われわれは正義を求めている。

立木　「正義を求めているが繁栄できない」という状態にあるわけですね。
　ただ、私たちとしては、日本が、イスラム教国と欧米諸国との間に立って、何とか仲介できるようにしたいと考えております。
　先般、鳩山さんがイランへ行き、いろいろと引っかき回していましたが……。

アフマディネジャド守護霊　鳩山さんは、君たち二人よりずっと親切で善人だったよ。

立木　（苦笑）ただ、日本国内では、鳩山さんはかなり評判を落としています。

1 An Interview with the Guardian Spirit of Mahmoud Ahmadinejad, President of Iran

Ahmadinejad's G.S. He is a representative of the Japanese gods, I think.

Tsuiki I really doubt that he is capable of reconciling the two countries.

Ahmadinejad's G.S. He is very kind! He has gentlemanship. He doesn't use rude words like you do.

Tsuiki Even if it hurts, I think a true friend would tell the truth.

From the perspective of Japan, Iran is…

Ahmadinejad's G.S. Please persuade the American president.

You, Japanese people suffered a lot from the great earthquake last year. And now, you are in a great confusion and you also need our oil.

第1章　イラン大統領・アフマディネジャド氏守護霊インタヴュー

アフマディネジャド守護霊　彼が"日本の神"の代表だと思うよ。

立木　鳩山さんでは、仲介役をするのは、ちょっと無理かと思います。

アフマディネジャド守護霊　彼は非常に親切だ。紳士(しんし)的だ。君のような無礼(ぶれい)な言葉は使わない。

立木　いや、本当の友人というのは、たまには、耳に痛いことも申し上げるものです。
　やはり、イランは、日本から見たら……。

アフマディネジャド守護霊　どうか、アメリカ大統領を説得してほしい。
　君たち日本人は、去年の大震災(だいしんさい)で、かなり苦しんだ。今は、大きな混乱のなかにあって、われわれの原油を必要としている。

You should not listen to the requests of the United States of America or European countries. You should decide for yourself. You need to be independent. You should import our oil through your own will, okay? Right?

And you need to persuade Barack Obama! Please say to him, "Barack Obama, you don't understand the Japanese position. You don't understand the right position to take."

He lacks love for Japanese people. He ate Japanese maccha (green tea) ice cream only in his younger days.

Tsuiki   I think that the U.S.-Japan Alliance is crucial for Japan's national interest, so even if Japan cannot help Iran at this moment, I hope that in the future, Japan could act as intermediary between Islamic countries and western countries.

第1章　イラン大統領・アフマディネジャド氏守護霊インタヴュー

　君たちは、アメリカ合衆国やヨーロッパ諸国の命令を聞くべきではない。自立すべきだ。自分自身の意思でもって、われわれから原油を輸入すべきだ。そうではないか。

　そして、バラク・オバマを説得するのだ。バラク・オバマに伝えてくれ。「あなたは、日本の立場、正しい立場が分かっていない」と。

　彼は、日本の人々への愛が欠けているよ。子供のときに、日本で抹茶アイスクリームを食べただけじゃないか。

立木　日本の国益を考えると、日米同盟を外すことはできませんので、そこを踏まえつつ、「今すぐ何かできるわけではないが、長い目で見て、欧米諸国とイスラム教国との仲介ができるようになりたい」と考えています。

1 An Interview with the Guardian Spirit of Mahmoud Ahmadinejad, President of Iran

Ahmadinejad's G.S.   You know Netanyahu?

You are planning to summon Prime Minister Netanyahu (his guardian spirit), next, right? Don't summon him! He is a devil, so please disregard him. He intends to attack, destroy, and kill all of us Iranian and Arabian people!

He is the devil of all devils!! You know?! More than Hitler!

11   We Hope Japan Will Be the Leader of the World

Ayaori   We will find that out for ourselves when we speak to Prime Minister Netanyahu's guardian spirit later.

I have one last question.

How do you feel about Happy Science spreading its teachings in Islamic countries?

アフマディネジャド守護霊　君はネタニヤフを知っているか。

　次は、彼（守護霊）を呼ぶつもりだろうが、彼を呼んではいけない。彼は悪魔だから、無視するんだ。彼は、われわれを攻撃し、破壊し、「イラン人とアラブ人全員を抹殺しよう」と考えている。

　こいつは、悪魔のなかの悪魔だ。分かっているのか。ヒトラー以上なんだぞ。

11　日本には「世界のリーダー」になってほしい

綾織　それについては、のちほど実際にお呼びして、確認してみます。

　最後に、もう一つ、質問させていただきます。
　幸福の科学がイスラム圏で伝道していくことについては、どのようにお考えですか。

1 An Interview with the Guardian Spirit of Mahmoud Ahmadinejad, President of Iran

Ahmadinejad's G.S.   It depends.

If you, the Happiness Realization Party, can persuade the U.S., as a real political party… if you can persuade Obama, then we can be friends, at that time. We should, we must, and we will be friends. I will accept you, recognize you, and appreciate you.

Tsuiki   Well, I think that Happy Science will spread as a religion widely, regardless of world politics.

Ayaori   We hope that Japan, as a country, will become more independent and be able to say our opinions to America.

Ahmadinejad's G.S.   You are so weak! Please be confident of your Japanese tradition, your splendid Japanese traditions!

We, Asian people, even the Middle Eastern people, look up to Japan!! Japan *must* be the leader of the

第1章　イラン大統領・アフマディネジャド氏守護霊インタヴュー

アフマディネジャド守護霊　状況次第だな。

　もし、君たち幸福実現党が本物の政党として、アメリカ合衆国を説得できたならば、オバマを説得できたならば、そのとき、われわれは友人になるし、そうなるべきだ。間違いない。われわれは仲間になる。私は、君たちのことを認め、称賛し、感謝するよ。

立木　ただ、宗教は宗教で、たぶん、どんどん広がっていくと思いますので。

綾織　将来的には、日本が独立した意思を持ち、アメリカに対しても、いろいろと発言できるようになると思います。

アフマディネジャド守護霊　君たちは非常に弱い。どうか、日本の素晴らしい伝統に自信を持ってほしい。

　われわれアジア人は、中東の人々でさえも、日本を尊敬しているのだ。日本は、世界のリーダーにならなけれ

91

1 An Interview with the Guardian Spirit of Mahmoud Ahmadinejad, President of Iran

world. (Making punching motions.) Japan must bash, slash, and throw punches at the United States, Germany, England, and France!

You have to fight!

Ayaori (Smiles wryly.) We won't be punching anybody, but I hope that Japan will become more independent and work as equals with western countries.

Tsuiki We hope that Japan will gain power as a nation, but we have no intention of fighting against the U.S. and European countries.

Ahmadinejad's G.S. You are so weak! No, no, no! Change, change, change!

Tsuiki No. We hope that Japan will become a strong nation that could lead the entire world.

ばならない(げんこつで殴るしぐさをする)。日本は、アメリカやドイツ、イギリス、フランスをめった切りにして、ぶん殴るべきだ。

　君たちは戦うべきである！

綾織　(苦笑)ぶん殴ったりはしませんが、独立した意思を持って、欧米諸国とも付き合いたいと思います。

立木　日本独自の国力をつけていきたいとは思いますが、「欧米と喧嘩をしたい」という考えはありません。

アフマディネジャド守護霊　君は弱い。駄目だ、駄目だ。替われ！ 交替だ！　チェインジ！

立木　いえいえ。私たちは、「日本を全世界が視野に入ったリーダーにしていきたい」と考えているのです。

1 An Interview with the Guardian Spirit of Mahmoud Ahmadinejad, President of Iran

Ayaori I hope that Japan will be actively involved in the issues of the Middle East and work to prevent wars from happening.

Ahmadinejad's G.S. You are so indecisive! No, no. That's not good.

Ayaori Thank you very much for coming today. I think we now have a good idea of how you think.

Ahmadinejad's G.S. You should write an article about our opinions. And when you do, you must write to persuade Prime Minister Noda not to cut the import quotation of crude oil from Iran. It's very important. Very, very, very important.

It's not good. Japan is an independent country. You should write. It should be the main opinion of your magazine.

第1章　イラン大統領・アフマディネジャド氏守護霊インタヴュー

綾織　中東の問題にも積極的にかかわり、戦争が避けられるように、何らかの役割を果たしていきたいと思います。

アフマディネジャド守護霊　君たちは優柔不断だ。駄目だな。よいことではない。

綾織　今日は、さまざまなご意見を頂き、まことにありがとうございました。よい参考になりました。

アフマディネジャド守護霊　君は、われわれの意見について、何か記事を書くべきだ。そのとき、野田首相がイランからの原油の輸入計画を削減しないように書いてくれ。これが非常に重要だ。

（削減は）よいことではない。日本は独立国家だ。君はそれを書くべきだし、それが君たちの雑誌の中心的な意見であるべきだ。

If you cannot write such an article, you should quit. (Pretends to cut his throat with his hand.) Quit!

Ayaori   I think that keeping our import quotation is one of our options, but it will depend on how much Iran is willing to compromise.

However, we will be printing your opinions in our magazine, *The Liberty*.

12   About Happy Science Activities in Iran

Ahmadinejad's G.S.   I am Mr. President. You should know that.

Ayaori   Thank you for coming today when you have such a busy schedule. Iran is going through some tough times, so perhaps it is better for you to return soon. Your country is waiting for your return.

第1章　イラン大統領・アフマディネジャド氏守護霊インタヴュー

　もし、そのような記事が書けないのならば、君は辞めるべきだ（手で首を切るしぐさをする）。辞めろ！

綾織　「輸入を削減しない」というのも一つの選択肢ですが、それは、イランがどのくらい妥協するかにもよると思います。
　ただ、ご意見自体は、「ザ・リバティ」誌上で発表させていただきます。

12　イランでの幸福の科学の活動をどう見ているか

アフマディネジャド守護霊　私は大統領だぞ。分かっているのか。

綾織　本日は、お忙しいなか、ありがとうございました。
　今、大変なときですので、早めにお帰りになったほうがよろしいかと思います。国のほうで待っていらっしゃると思いますので……。

1 An Interview with the Guardian Spirit of Mahmoud Ahmadinejad, President of Iran

Ahmadinejad's G.S. I've heard that you sent some Happy Science people from Japan on a mission, a crusade; we can kill them, you know!

Ayaori I hope that Happy Science can continue its activities while cooperating with Islam.

Ahmadinejad's G.S. Okay. But, there is no justice in you.

Ayaori We will make efforts so Iran can continue to exist.

Ahmadinejad's G.S. Oh! No, no, no, no, no, within a few years, we will be massacred by that bad country.

Ayaori We will try to prevent that from happening

第1章　イラン大統領・アフマディネジャド氏守護霊インタヴュー

アフマディネジャド守護霊　「幸福の科学の伝道師が、数名、日本からわが国に送り込まれている」と聞いている。われわれは、彼らを処刑することもできるのだ。それを分かっているのか。

綾織　いえいえ。私たちは、イスラム教とも協調しながら活動していきたいと思っているのです。

アフマディネジャド守護霊　分かった。しかし、君のなかには正義がない。

綾織　私たちは、イランの存続のためにも努力してまいりたいと思います。

アフマディネジャド守護霊　ああ、いやいや。数年以内に、われわれは、悪い国から大虐殺される。

綾織　それを避けられるように、努力してまいりたいと

Ahmadinejad's G.S. Really? Really?

I think that you want to join the other countries, like the United States of America.

Are you sure that your Japanese defense army will not come to our country and assist them in something, hm?

Ayaori It is part of our mission to prevent humankind's final war, so I hope to work together with Iranians.

Ahmadinejad's G.S. Okay. Okay.

Hmm….You have some people in Iran. So please pray for them, for their peaceful return.

Tsuiki I think that, from a western perspective, you are too restricting. You should at least guarantee

第1章　イラン大統領・アフマディネジャド氏守護霊インタヴュー

思います。

アフマディネジャド守護霊　本当か。本気か。
　君たちは、かの国々に加わりたいのだろう？　私はそう思っているよ。
　日本の自衛隊は、アメリカ合衆国の軍隊とともに、わが国に入ってきて、何か、アメリカの支援をするつもりではないのか。どうなのだ？

綾織　「最終戦争を避ける」というのが、私たちの使命でもあります。ぜひ、イランの人々とも協力していきたいと思います。

アフマディネジャド守護霊　本当か。よし、いいだろう。
　イランにいる君たちの仲間のために祈ることだ。「彼らが無事に帰還できるように」とな。

立木　そのあたりの意識が、欧米の感覚からすると、少し行きすぎに見えるのではないでしょうか。やはり、移

101

people the freedom to travel.

Ahmadinejad's G.S.   If they are spying, we cannot accept them.

Tsuiki   They are not spies. They have a religious mission and are trying to convey the truth of God. I hope that you will be more understanding of Happy Science.

Ahmadinejad's G.S.   No permission granted. You said nothing that will be for our good.

Ayaori   We will make efforts to reconcile Israel and Iran.

Thank you for coming today.

Tsuiki   Thank you very much.

動の自由などは、きちんと確保すべきだと思います。

アフマディネジャド守護霊　もし、彼らがスパイ活動をしているならば、われわれは、彼らを受け入れることができない。

立木　いいえ、スパイではありません。彼らは宗教的なミッションを持ち、神の真実を伝えるために活動しているので、ご容赦いただきたいと思います。

アフマディネジャド守護霊　許可しない。君たちは、われわれのためになることを何も言わなかった。

綾織　イスラエルとイランが最終的に和解できるよう、私たちも努力していきたいと思います。
　本日は、本当にありがとうございました。

立木　ありがとうございました。

1 An Interview with the Guardian Spirit of Mahmoud Ahmadinejad, President of Iran

Ahmadinejad's G.S. Okay. Bye! (Waves good-bye.)

Okawa This is going to be a tough one.

第1章　イラン大統領・アフマディネジャド氏守護霊インタヴュー

アフマディネジャド守護霊　分かった。じゃあな(手を振る)。

大川隆法　うーん、これは難しいですね。

Chapter Two:
An Interview with the Guardian Spirit of Benjamin Netanyahu, Prime Minister of Israel

April 17, 2012, at the Tokyo Headquarters of Happy Science
Spiritual Messages from the Guardian Spirit of Benjamin Netanyahu

第2章
イスラエル首相・ネタニヤフ氏 守護霊インタヴュー

2012年4月17日 幸福の科学総合本部にて
ベンヤミン・ネタニヤフ守護霊の霊示

Benjamin Netanyahu (1949～)

Current Prime Minister of Israel. He studied architecture at the Massachusetts Institute of Technology, business administration at the MIT Sloan School of Management, and political science at MIT and Harvard University. After being employed at Boston Consulting Group, he served as ambassador to the UN before entering politics. Served three years as Prime Minister from 1996 but withdrew after a corruption scandal. He returned to politics in 2002 as Foreign Minister and became Prime Minister in the 2009 parliamentary election in which he campaigned against Iran's nuclear development program.

ベンヤミン・ネタニヤフ（1949〜）

イスラエル国首相。マサチューセッツ工科大学（MIT）で建築学、同スローン経営大学院で経営管理を学び、さらにハーバード大学とMITで政治学を学ぶ。ボストン・コンサルティング・グループ勤務や国連大使等を経て、政界に進出。1996年から3年間、首相を務めたが、汚職疑惑により、一時的に政界を引退。2002年、外相として政界に復帰し、2009年総選挙では「イランの核武装阻止」等を訴え、首相に再登板した。

1 Summoning the Guardian Spirit of the Israeli Prime Minister

Okawa We will now summon the Israeli Prime Minister, Mr. Netanyahu's guardian spirit. According to his background, he seems to be a very intellectual person and tough to speak with.

Let us begin.

I will now summon him.

(Puts hands in prayer and closes eyes. About 45 seconds of silence.)

Tsuiki Hello. Are you the guardian spirit of the Israeli Prime Minister, Mr. Netanyahu?

Netanyahu's Guardian Spirit* Um? Yeah, yeah.

---

* Netanyahu's Guardian Spirit will be noted as Netanyahu's G.S. from this point on.

第2章　イスラエル首相・ネタニヤフ氏守護霊インタヴュー

1　イスラエル首相の守護霊を招霊する

大川隆法　次は、イスラエルのネタニヤフ首相です。
　この人は、経歴を見るかぎり、インテリのようですね。かなりのインテリなので、こちらも手強そうです。

　それでは行きますか。
　では、イスラエル首相、ベンヤミン・ネタニヤフ氏の守護霊をお呼びしたいと思います。

（合掌し、瞑目する。約45秒間の沈黙）

立木　こんにちは。イスラエルのネタニヤフ首相の守護霊様でいらっしゃいますでしょうか。

ネタニヤフ守護霊　ん？　ああ、そうだが。

111

Tsuiki   Thank you for coming to the Tokyo Headquarters of Happy Science.

Netanyahu's G.S.   What can I do for you?

Tsuiki   My name is Tsuiki. I am the head of the Happiness Realization Party, a political party in Japan.

Netanyahu's G.S.   Ah, Tsuiki. Tsu-ee-Ki. Okay. Tsuiki, Okay. I got it.

2 He Is Thinking of Attacking Iran As Soon As Today

Tsuiki   Iran's nuclear development is creating tensions with Israel. Since Japan imports crude oil from Iran, this issue between Israel and Iran will directly affect us. Prime Minister Netanyahu is the other party involved in this issue, so we have invited you, his

立木　本日は、幸福の科学総合本部にお越しくださいまして、ありがとうございます。

ネタニヤフ守護霊　何か用かね？

立木　私は、日本の幸福実現党の党首を務めている立木と申します。

ネタニヤフ守護霊　ああ、立木ね。立木。分かった。立木ね。

2　「今日にでもイランを攻撃したい」が本音

立木　今、イランの核開発問題をめぐり、イスラエルとの関係が非常に緊迫しております。これは、日本にとっても、原油の輸入などで、直接、影響を受ける問題ですので、ぜひ、その一方の主役であるネタニヤフ首相の守護霊様に、今のお考えをお訊きしたいと考え、こちらに

2 An Interview with the Guardian Spirit of Benjamin Netanyahu, Prime Minister of Israel

guardian spirit, today to find out your opinions.

According to recent news, you have made it clear that you cannot overlook Iran's nuclear development. In regards to your timing of attack, I think you have stated that, "It is not a matter of days or weeks, but also not a matter of years. (If Iran continues its nuclear development) We are ready to strike Iranian nuclear sites within the next few months." When exactly do you plan to launch this attack?

Netanyahu's G.S. My wish is to do it today. They are similar to North Korea. They're almost the same. They are like North Korea for you.

Tsuiki I have heard that Iran is trading military technology with North Korea.

Netanyahu's G.S. For us, they are like North Korea. They're crazy!

第2章　イスラエル首相・ネタニヤフ氏守護霊インタヴュー

お呼びしました。

　最近の報道によりますと、首相は、「イランの核開発は見過ごせない。数日、数週間とは言わないまでも、数年以上は待てない。（開発をやめない場合は）数カ月以内にイランの核施設(しせつ)を攻撃(こうげき)することができる」というような意思を表明されていますが、実際には、いつごろの攻撃を考えておられるのでしょうか。

ネタニヤフ守護霊　私の希望としては、今日にでも攻撃したいね。彼らは、北朝鮮(きたちょうせん)と似ている。ほとんど同じだ。つまり、彼らは、君たちにとっての北朝鮮なんだよ。

立木　確かに、「北朝鮮とイランには技術的な交流もある」と聞いております。

ネタニヤフ守護霊　われわれにとって、彼らは"北朝鮮"だ。キチガイなんだよ！

115

3 Has the U.S. Navy Fleet Agreed to Assist Israel?

Tsuiki However, thinking realistically, there are several difficult factors in attacking Iran's nuclear facilities, as there is a distance of about 2,000 km between Iran and Israel. You would have to refuel your combat aircrafts somewhere if you were to use them.

Moreover, because their nuclear facilities are deep underground, it makes it extremely difficult to destroy them. What kind of attack plan do you exactly have in mind?

Netanyahu's G.S. I talked to Mr. Obama about that. The U.S. Seventh Fleet will assist us. [Note]
p.120

Tsuiki You mean that the U.S. will assist you? Have

第2章　イスラエル首相・ネタニヤフ氏守護霊インタヴュー

3　「米艦隊が支援する」との合意が
　　なされた？

立木　ただ、実際に攻撃する場合には、両国間の距離は2000キロ近く離れているため、戦闘機の給油をしなければならない等、さまざまな技術的な困難があります。

　また、イランの核開発の工場は地下深くにあり、攻撃の際に、かなりの困難も予想されるのですが、これについては、すでに何か対策を打っておられるのでしょうか。

ネタニヤフ守護霊　それについては、オバマ氏と話したよ。米軍の第7艦隊が、われわれを支援してくれることになっている。[注]
p.121

立木　「米軍が助けてくれる」ということですか。それは

117

they already agreed to help you?

Netanyahu's G.S.   Yeah, yeah. He said that it's okay. It's okay. But before that, we must negotiate with them peacefully, and we will also need agreements from other countries. It's important, I think. But I predict that our victory is one hundred percent sure.

Tsuiki   You said earlier that Iran is similar to North Korea. However, I think that Iran fears Israel because Israel already owns nuclear weapons. I feel that Iran is developing nuclear weapons to defend themselves from Israel's capability to attack. Would you agree with me?

Netanyahu's G.S.   Umm…hmmmm.

Tsuiki   Japan's relationship with North Korea is different from yours with Iran. Japan has never owned

すでに合意がなされたのでしょうか。

ネタニヤフ守護霊　そう、そう。だから大丈夫だ。大丈夫。ただ、その前に、われわれは、彼らと平和裡に交渉しなければならない。世界の他の国々の合意も必要だ。それが大事だと思うね。しかし、われわれの勝利は、100パーセント確実だ。そう予想している。

立木　いま、「イランは北朝鮮と同じだ」という見解を示されましたが、イランとしては、イスラエルがすでに核兵器を持っているために、非常に怯えているのではないでしょうか。つまり、「イスラエルに何とか対抗しなければいけない」と考えて、核開発を進めている面もあると思うのですが、これについてはいかがでしょうか。

ネタニヤフ守護霊　うーん。

立木　日本と北朝鮮の場合、「日本が核兵器を持っていないにもかかわらず、北朝鮮は、勝手に核開発を行い、ど

nuclear weapons. However, North Korea continues to develop their nuclear weapons and missile technology. This is the difference between Iran and North Korea.

Netanyahu's G.S. Ahh, you mean the double standard. We hold the sacred place of Christianity, so the people of Europe and the United States want to protect us; it's because of Jesus Christ. That is our strong point. They are afraid of losing the birthplace of Jesus Christ. That is our strong point.

> [Note] Strictly speaking, the U.S. Fifth Fleet is now in charge of the Middle East. However, most of its operating forces and facilities are rotationally deployed to the region from either the Pacific Fleet including the Seventh Fleet or the Atlantic Fleet. The Guardian Spirit of Netanyafu seemingly made

んどんミサイルを発射している」という状況があります。この点において、「北朝鮮とイランには違いがある」と思われますが。

ネタニヤフ守護霊　つまり、二重基準があるということかね？　しかし、イスラエルには、キリスト教の聖地がある。だから、ヨーロッパやアメリカの人々は、イエス・キリストのために、われわれを守らなければならない。それがわれわれの強みだ。彼らは、イエス・キリストの生誕地を失うのを恐れているからね。それがわれわれの強みだ。

　［注］厳密に言えば、現在、中東は「第5艦隊」が担当している。ただし、第5艦隊は、第7艦隊を含む太平洋艦隊および大西洋艦隊からの人員や機材の提供を受けて編成される。ここでのネタニヤフ守護霊の発言は、状況に応じて第7艦隊の艦船が中東に派遣されていることを受けてのものと思われる。

his comment in response to the fact that ships from the Seventh Fleet are deployed to the Middle East, if required.

4 Judaism and Islam Should Be Able to Coexist under the Supreme God

Tsuiki   Would it be possible for Christians and Muslims to share or have joint control over Jerusalem?

Netanyahu's G.S.   No, no. It's difficult, difficult, difficult, very difficult. History has already proven this. What I mean is that Jerusalem must be the sacred place of Christianity. Also, the Jewish people make up the mother nation of Christians. That's why we stay together, and we are one. We have the same roots, and the same sacred place.

第2章　イスラエル首相・ネタニヤフ氏守護霊インタヴュー

4 唯一の至高神がいれば、
　　ユダヤとイスラムは愛し合えるはず

立木　そうすると、キリスト教とイスラム教の間で何らかの調停をし、「エルサレムを共同管理する」などということはできないのでしょうか。

ネタニヤフ守護霊　いやいや、それは難しいよ。難しい。とても困難なことだ。それは歴史が証明している。つまり、エルサレムはキリスト教の聖地でなければならないし、ユダヤはキリスト教徒の母国でもある。したがって、われわれは緊密であり、一体であり、同じルーツ、同じ聖地を持っているのだ。

So we must fight against evil countries by gathering our powers.

Tsuiki   The Happiness Realization Party is affiliated with a religion called Happy Science. Happy Science teaches that the Fundamental God of Christianity and Judaism, and the Fundamental God of Islam, Allah, are actually the same being named Elohim. Elohim's real name is El Cantare. Such truths have been revealed at Happy Science.

Netanyahu's G.S.   Umm... Hmmm...(Thinking deeply.)

Tsuiki   So in short, while it seems like there are many different religions in this world, all religions actually come from the same God.

Since Christians, Jewish people, and Muslims ultimately believe in the same God, religious wars

第2章　イスラエル首相・ネタニヤフ氏守護霊インタヴュー

　だから、われわれは、力を合わせて、悪(あ)しき国々と戦わなければならない。

立木　私ども幸福実現党は、ハッピー・サイエンス（幸福の科学）という宗教が母体なのですが、その教えのなかで、「実は、キリスト教とユダヤ教の根源の神と、イスラム教の根源の神、すなわちアッラーは、最終的には、『エローヒム』という一つの存在に行き着く。その本当の名は『エル・カンターレ』である」という真実が明かされています。

ネタニヤフ守護霊　うーん。

立木　要するに、「同じ神の下(もと)で、たまたま違(ちが)う宗教になっている」ということです。

　キリスト教、ユダヤ教、イスラム教とも、究極的には「同じ神」を信じているのであれば、それぞれの宗教の信

125

and conflicts are meaningless. If all people could embrace this understanding, it would be possible for all religions to coexist peacefully.

Netanyahu's G.S. It's one hypothesis, and we cannot prove that. We cannot determine whether or not Allah and our God are the same, the same Supreme Being. It's a very difficult matter, and we have been fighting about it for more than 2,000 years, or at least for 1,400 years. So, it's not so easy.

If it is true that our Gods are the same, and only one God, we can love each other; Islamic people and Jewish people can love each other. But both sides have been fighting under the name of "God." Then, that must mean that the simple prerequisite for this conflict must be the existence of two gods. This is a simple answer for that phenomenon.

Tsuiki There are various gods existing under the

者同士が戦争をすることは、ある意味で、非常に虚しいといえます。したがって、その教えを受け入れれば、「平和的な共存は可能になる」と考えるのですが。

ネタニヤフ守護霊　それは、一つの仮説にしかすぎないな。われわれは、それを証明できない。アッラーとわれわれの神が同じ至高の存在であるかどうかは、われわれには決められない。それは非常に難しい問題であるし、われわれは2000年以上、あるいは最低でも1400年以上は戦っているんだ。だから、そんなに簡単なことではない。

　もし、神が同じ存在で、一人しかいないのであれば、われわれは、つまりイスラム教徒とユダヤ教徒は、お互いに愛し合えるはずではないか。しかし、実際には、同じ「神」の名の下で戦っている。つまり、この紛争における単純な前提としては、「二つの神がいるはずだ」ということになる。それが、この現象を説明する簡単な答えだ。

立木　その原因は、要するに、「『一なる神』のすぐ下に

Supreme God. The religious wars and conflicts that are happening now are caused by disparities in the spirits' opinions and thinking.

Netanyahu's G.S. I don't think so. If only one Supreme God, an existence that we cannot explain or describe through words, exists, then that Supreme Being should be able to persuade other angels or higher spirits. He can. And he should persuade other higher beings. It's impossible that higher spirits or angels could be fighting each other and disregarding the Will of God. It's impossible.

5 Is Yahweh Truly the Supreme God?

Ayaori I know you are not allowed to call God by His name, but do you believe that Yahweh is God?

いる神々の間で、少し"見解の相違"があるために、今、いろいろな紛争が起きている」ということです。

ネタニヤフ守護霊　そうは思わないね。もし、唯一の至高神がいるのであれば、彼は、「彼」と呼んでいいのかは分からないが、あるいは言葉を超えた存在かもしれないが、そのような至高の存在は、他の天使や高級霊を説得できるはずだよ。あるいは、他の上位霊を説得すべきだと思うね。そうすれば、高級霊や天使が、神の意思を無視して戦うようなことなど、ありえないはずだ。

5　ヤハウェは本当に至高神なのか

綾織　一つ質問なのですが、あなたが想定している「神」とは、名前で呼ぶのは難しいかもしれませんけれども、「ヤハウェ」ということでよろしいでしょうか。

Netanyahu's G.S. Ah, yeah, Yahweh. No, in truth, there is no name for God. Yahweh is a secret code.

Ayaori I believe Yahweh is not the Supreme God but a regional god that only guides the Jewish people.

Netanyahu's G.S. Uh?

Ayaori We believe that Yahweh is only an ethnic god watching over the Jewish people.

Netanyahu's G.S. The Supreme God made us, Jewish people, and then other people. We are the origin of the human race.

Tsuiki However, the Jewish people have wandered about for nearly two thousand years and have had an

ネタニヤフ守護霊　ああ、そうだ。ヤハウェだ。いや、実際には、神に名前などない。ヤハウェというのは、シークレット・コード（秘密の暗号）なのだ。

綾織　ヤハウェは最高神というわけではなく、どちらかというと、ユダヤ民族を指導している神であるかと思うのですが。

ネタニヤフ守護霊　ん？

綾織　私たちは、ヤハウェを、「ユダヤ民族の神」として認識しているのです。

ネタニヤフ守護霊　至高神が、われわれユダヤ人を創られたのだ。それから、他の民族ができた。われわれは人類の祖先なのだ。

立木　ただ、ユダヤ民族は、「2000年近くも放浪する」という、非常につらい歴史をお持ちです。したがって、そ

extremely difficult past. If they were truly led by the "Supreme God," I don't think they would have gone through such tragic experiences.

Netanyahu's G.S. No, no. Adam and Eve are Jewish. Ha, ha, ha!

Tsuiki The story of Adam and Eve was actually based on myths of the Middle East.

Netanyahu's G.S. You, too. You are the descendants of Jewish souls. Even Japanese people are Jewish.

Tsuiki I don't think that the regional god of the Jewish people is the Supreme God.

Netanyahu's G.S. No. Believe it.

のような民族の神様が「スプリーム」（至高）かどうかについては、やや疑問があります。

ネタニヤフ守護霊　いやいや、アダムとイヴは、ユダヤ人だった。ハハハ。

立木　その神話についても、中東のいろいろな神話がベースになっているわけです。

ネタニヤフ守護霊　君たちは、ユダヤ人の魂の子孫なのだよ。日本人でさえ、元はユダヤ人だ。

立木　「ユダヤ民族の神」が、そのまま、「スプリームゴッド」（至高神）と言えるかどうか、やや疑問の余地はあります。

ネタニヤフ守護霊　違う。信じよ。

Tsuiki   We believe that there are many gods guiding the various ethnic groups and religions. These spirits are competing against each other, just as companies compete against each other in business. However, there is a Supreme God who stands above all gods and deities.

Unfortunately, this competition between the gods has also caused religious wars and conflicts. I understand that the conflict between Israel and Iran is caused by this competition between the gods as well.

Netanyahu′s G.S.   No, that is a misunderstanding. Gods don't compete. Only God and the devil compete against each other. And we are on the side of God. We belong to God and they belong to the devil. That's the simple conclusion.

第2章　イスラエル首相・ネタニヤフ氏守護霊インタヴュー

立木　私どもの教えでは、「いろいろな民族や宗教の神が存在し、企業間競争のように、神々の間で一種の競争を行うことによって、切磋琢磨をしている。さらに、その上に"究極の神"がいる」という見方をしています。

そして、そうした競争の過程で、残念ながら、宗教戦争が発生するわけです。今、イスラエルとイランが対立しているのは、そういう理由によるものと理解しています。

ネタニヤフ守護霊　いや、それは誤解だ。神は競争しない。神と悪魔だけが競争するんだ。そして、われわれは神に属するから、彼ら（イラン）は悪魔に属することになる。それが単純な結論だ。

135

6 Is Netanyahu's Guardian Spirit St. Michael's Soul Mate?

Ayaori So, as the prime minister's guardian spirit, what sort of spirits do you interact with normally?

For example, St. Michael, one of Israel's gods, is also involved in Christianity…

Netanyahu's G.S. St. Michael? St. Michael, yeah. And the Islamic people insist that they were guided by St. Gabriel. But St. Michael has a higher position than St. Gabriel. So they should obey us.

Ayaori Do you have connections with these spirits?

Netanyahu's G.S. Yeah, I'm a friend of St. Michael. Yeah, yeah.

6 ネタニヤフ守護霊は
　　聖ミカエルのソウルメイト？

綾織　話は変わりますが、あなたは、ネタニヤフ首相の守護霊様ですけれども、霊界では、普段、どういう方と話をされているのでしょうか。

　例えば、イスラエルの神である「ミカエル」という存在は、キリスト教にもかかわっているわけですが……。

ネタニヤフ守護霊　聖ミカエルだ。そうだよ。イスラム教徒は「聖ガブリエルに指導された」と言い張っているが、聖ミカエルのほうが、聖ガブリエルよりも高い地位にある。だから、彼らは、われわれに従わなければならない。

綾織　そういう方々と、普段、何か接点はありますか。

ネタニヤフ守護霊　そうだ。私は、聖ミカエルの友人だよ。そう、そう。

Ayaori He's your friend?

Netanyahu's G.S. Believe me, believe me.

Ayaori When you reincarnate onto earth, are you always born as a Jewish person?

Netanyahu's G.S. Maybe, I am a soul mate of St. Michael.

Ayaori (Laughs.) If that were true, Israel would completely defeat Iran.

Netanyahu's G.S. St. Michael is a god of fighting, right? So, I will destroy the fortress of evil spirits.

Ayaori When we conducted St. Michael's spiritual messages, St. Michael said that Muhammad was a High Spirit living in Heaven and not a devil.

綾織　友達なのですか。

ネタニヤフ守護霊　信じなさい。私を信じなさい。

綾織　あなた自身は、常にユダヤ民族のなかで生まれてきた魂なのですか。

ネタニヤフ守護霊　あるいは、聖ミカエルのソウルメイトかもしれないね。

綾織　（笑）それが真実であれば、イランに「完全勝利」するのでしょうけれども……。

ネタニヤフ守護霊　聖ミカエルは、戦の神だろう？　だから、私は悪霊の要塞を破壊するのだ。

立木　ただ、幸福の科学の霊査によると、ミカエルは、ムハンマドについては、悪魔ではなく、「天上界にいる高級霊である」という認識でいらっしゃるようなのですが。

Netanyahu's G.S. No, no. Muhammad is a devil.

Tsuiki Is that how you understand Muhammad?

Netanyahu's G.S. I am 100 % sure! He is a devil. He was a devil! He is a devil! He will be a devil!

Tsuiki Since you believe that Muhammad is a devil, we know for a fact that you are not part of St. Michael's soul.

Netanyahu's G.S. Islam is a bad religion!

(『世界紛争の真実』第2章参照)

ネタニヤフ守護霊　いや、違う。ムハンマドは悪魔だ。

立木　しかし、そう認識しておられるということは……。

ネタニヤフ守護霊　彼は100パーセント悪魔だ。過去も悪魔であったし、今も悪魔だし、これからも悪魔だ。

立木　ただ、われわれとしては、あなたがそのような認識に基づく見解を示すこと自体で、「おそらくミカエルの魂ではない」と判定できるのです。

ネタニヤフ守護霊　イスラム教は、悪い宗教だ。

7 The Reason Why Judaism Won't Spread around the World

Tsuiki However, if we strictly look at the number of believers, there are over one billion Muslims while there are only 7.5 million people in Israel.

Netanyahu's G.S. They are… you know, you know, Muhammad is a god of gangs! He is a godfather of gangs! The mafia! You know them?

Tsuiki If God really did exist, He would never allow over one billion people to become members of a gang or mafia.

Netanyahu's G.S. Bad things spread more easily. You are a good religion? So you cannot spread your teachings. If you are a bad religion, your teachings will spread faster than the new trunk line in Japan. Right?

7 ユダヤ教が全世界に広がらない理由

立木 しかし、信者の数で言えば、イスラム教は10億人以上いるわけです。それに対し、イスラエルの人口は750万人です。

ネタニヤフ守護霊 彼らは……、ほら、あれだよ、ムハンマドは暴力団の神だ。暴力団というか、マフィアのゴッドファーザーだ。分かるか？

立木 ただ、本当に神がいらっしゃるのであれば、ギャングやマフィアの信者が10億人以上も発生するような状況を捨ててはおかないと思いますよ。

ネタニヤフ守護霊 悪いものは、簡単に広がるんだよ。君たちは良い宗教なんだろう？ だから、教えを広げられずにいるんだ。もし、君たちが悪い宗教なら、日本の新幹線よりも早く、教えが広まるよ。そうだろう？

Tsuiki   We are hoping to spread Happy Science to all humankind.

Netanyahu's G.S.   Since we are a good religion, we have only eight million followers. That's because we're a very good religion with supreme contents in our teachings. That is the reason for the difficulty in spreading the Truths. If we have more power, we can teach Christians. They just misunderstood our real concept of God.

So, we can persuade them if we have more power. And then, our new Jewish teachings can prevail on Earth again.

Tsuiki   However, I think that your lack of power to spread the Jewish teachings shows that your god has very limited power.

第2章　イスラエル首相・ネタニヤフ氏守護霊インタヴュー

立木　われわれは、全人類に対して教えを広げていきたいと思っています。

ネタニヤフ守護霊　われわれは、良い宗教であり続けている。だから、800万人しか信者がいないんだ。われわれの教えは素晴らしく、最高の内容だから、それを広げるのが難しいのだ。われわれにもっと力があれば、キリスト教徒にも教えることができる。彼らは、われわれの本当の神の概念を誤解しているからね。

　だから、もし、われわれにもっと力があれば、彼らを説得し、新たなユダヤの教えを、再び地上に行き渡らせることができるのだ。

立木　ただ、あなたがたに、「ユダヤの教えを広げるだけの力がない」ということは、やはり、「信じている神にも力がない」ということなのではないでしょうか。

Netanyahu's G.S. No, no, no. Good things are very difficult to spread. You've already experienced that. Right?

Ayaori I don't agree with you. The god that you are speaking of only seems to have influence over the Jewish people.

Netanyahu's G.S. No, no, no, no, no. Do you have eight million followers in Japan? Right? Really?

Ayaori Well, we now know your perspectives.

Netanyahu's G.S. Uh, huh. And it's Elohim? Really?

ネタニヤフ守護霊　いやいや、違う。良いものは、とても広がりにくいんだ。それを君たちも経験したのだろう？

綾織　それは少し違います。やはり、あなたがたの信じる神の力は、ユダヤ民族に限られているのではないかと思います。

ネタニヤフ守護霊　いやいや、絶対に違う。それなら、君たちには、日本に800万人の信者がいるのかい？　どうだ？

綾織　あなたの考え方は非常によく分かりました。

ネタニヤフ守護霊　それでエローヒムなのかい？　本当に？

8 What Is the True Justice of God?

Ayaori   According to you, there are many countries in the Middle East that must be eliminated.

Netanyahu's G.S.   True, that's true. Because they belong to devils. So we must save them! It is the great deed of Saviors. I'm a savior of the Middle East.

Ayaori   Islam is gaining influence in Egypt and the countries surrounding Egypt. All of those countries will become your enemies.

Netanyahu's G.S.   No, no, no, no. They are under the power of devils. So we must change their mind towards a good direction. They must seek God, the real God!

第2章　イスラエル首相・ネタニヤフ氏守護霊インタヴュー

8　本当の「神の正義」はどこにあるのか

綾織　あなたのお考えでいった場合、今後、中東は「滅ぼさなければいけない国」ばかりになってしまうわけですが……。

ネタニヤフ守護霊　そうだ、そのとおりだ。彼らは、悪魔に属しているんだからな。彼らを救わなければならない。これは、救世主の偉業である。私は、中東の救世主なのだ。

綾織　今後、エジプトもイスラム化していくでしょうし、その他の周辺国も、かなりイスラム主義的な方向性で進んでいくと思うのです。そうなると、それらの国々をすべて敵に回すことになりますよ。

ネタニヤフ守護霊　違う、違う。彼らは、悪魔の勢力だ。だから、われわれは、彼らの心を良い方向に変えなければならない。彼らは、神を求めなければならない。本物の神をだ。

149

Tsuiki Israel is occupying the West Bank of the Jordan River and many Islamic Palestinians are being violently evicted from their homes by the Israeli settlers and military. How should we interpret such actions?

Netanyahu's G.S. Hmmm?

Tsuiki You are driving out Palestinians to increase the settlements of Jewish people in the West Bank. I've heard that Israel's army is sweeping out the Palestinians. In light of God's justice, I believe you are overdoing it.

Netanyahu's G.S. Hmm…Hmmm. It's very doubtful whether Happy Science is a real religion or not, then. You have too much sympathy with the bad religion of Islam. It's not good. It's not the global

第2章　イスラエル首相・ネタニヤフ氏守護霊インタヴュー

立木　ただ、イスラエルは、パレスチナのヨルダン川西岸などを占領していますが、この地域で、「パレスチナのイスラム教徒たちを、虐殺に近いかたちで、どんどん追いやっている」とも聞いています。これは、どのように理解すればよいのでしょうか。

ネタニヤフ守護霊　ん？

立木　つまり、この地域に、どんどんユダヤ人を入植させる一方で、「イスラエル軍を使って、パレスチナ人を掃討している」とも聞いているのですが、私どもは、「本当の『神の正義』ということを考えれば、これはやりすぎではないか」と見ています。

ネタニヤフ守護霊　うーむ。幸福の科学が「本物の宗教」なのかどうか、かなり疑わしいね。君たちは、イスラム教という悪い宗教に共感しすぎている。それは良くない。世界標準ではない。そのような考えは捨てたまえ。

151

standard. Please abandon that kind of thought.

Ayaori We are siding with neither Islam nor Judaism.

Netanyahu's G.S. No. Taking that standpoint is very dangerous.

Ayaori We are aiming to reconcile both religions, so we will not take sides.

Netanyahu's G.S. God and the devil have been fighting several thousand years. Even God never reconciles, so neither will we.

Ayaori In the Old Testament, there is a god named Yahweh, but there is also a god named Elohim. I think that it would be better for the Jewish people to follow the teachings of Elohim, who is more compassionate.

綾織　われわれは、イスラム教側とユダヤ教側のどちらか一方に立っているわけではありません。

ネタニヤフ守護霊　いや、その立場は、かなり危険だ。

綾織　両者の宗教の和解を目指しておりますので、どちら側ということではないのです。

ネタニヤフ守護霊　神と悪魔は何千年も戦っている。神でさえ、決して妥協することはない。したがって、われわれも妥協しない。

綾織　『旧約聖書』には、「ヤハウェ」という存在も出てきますが、「エローヒム」という存在も登場します。ですから、ユダヤの民にとっては、より寛容な神の考えに従っていくのが最善の道なのではないかと思いますよ。

Netanyahu's G.S. If Elohim is guiding the Islamic people now, then our God will fight against Elohim. We cannot bear taking that kind of a middle way. Your middle way cannot be accepted. What is right, is right. What is bad, is bad.

9 A Deeply Rooted Mistrust towards Islam

Ayaori I hope to spread Happy Science teachings to Jewish people so they can change their way of thinking.

I can guess how you might answer, but what do you think about Happy Science teachings spreading in Israel?

Netanyahu's G.S. It's impossible! Impossible.

第 2 章　イスラエル首相・ネタニヤフ氏守護霊インタヴュー

ネタニヤフ守護霊　もし、エローヒムが、今、イスラム教徒を指導しているのなら、われわれの神はエローヒムと戦うだろう。われわれは、そのような"中道"には耐えられない。君たちの中道の考え方は受け入れられない。正しいものは正しい。悪いものは悪いのだ。

9　イスラム教に対する根深い不信感

綾織　今後、ハッピー・サイエンスとしても、ユダヤの方々の考え方を少し変えていただけるように、教えを伝えていきたいと思っています。

　そこで、これから質問しようと思っていることについては、だいたい答えの予想がついてしまうのですが、イスラエルにハッピー・サイエンスの教えが広がっていくことについては、どのようにお考えでしょうか。

ネタニヤフ守護霊　それは不可能だ。不可能。無理だね。

Impossible.

Tsuiki　I think the Israeli people are distressed and their minds are not at peace because they are constantly fighting their neighbors.

Netanyahu's G.S.　Ha, ha, ha, ha, ha.

Tsuiki　In that sense, a religious reconciliation is extremely important for the Israeli people to find peace of mind.

Netanyahu's G.S.　Can you live with cockroaches? It's difficult.

Tsuiki　Both Judaism and Islam are religions that were founded hundreds or even thousands of years ago. I don't think that even the religious leaders at the

第2章　イスラエル首相・ネタニヤフ氏守護霊インタヴュー

立木　ただ、イスラエルの方々は、日夜、ある種の臨戦態勢に置かれて生活しておられますので、かなりストレスが多く、心の状態としては非常に厳しいのではないかと思うのです。

ネタニヤフ守護霊　ハハハ。

立木　そういう意味で、「心の平和」を取り戻すためにも、やはり、宗教の和解は非常に大事ではないでしょうか。

ネタニヤフ守護霊　君たちは、ゴキブリと一緒に住めるのかね？　それは難しいことだよ。

立木　ただ、ユダヤ教やイスラム教は、それぞれ、数千年あるいは千数百年もたっている昔の教えですから、必ずしも、その当時の宗教指導者の方々がすべてを分かっ

time had a complete understanding of the teachings.

In this meaning, I think that it is necessary to give new teachings that are suitable for today's world.

Netanyahu's G.S. Never forget the US-Japan alliance. You shouldn't forget about that, hm?

Tsuiki Of course, it is important to keep the alliance, but Japan has opinions of its own. We hope to keep the alliance as a sturdy foundation for Japan, but we also wish that Japan, as a country, can influence America.

The people of Israel are actively lobbying to increase their influence in the United States. This is something that we must learn from the Israelis.

However, the worldviews of Christianity and Judaism do not cover the entire world, so in that sense the two religions are limited as to what they can do.

ていたわけではないと思うのです。
　そういう意味では、やはり、「現在の地球の状態に応じた教え」が新たに展開されるべきです。

ネタニヤフ守護霊　「日米同盟」を決して忘れるなよ。それを忘れるな。

立木　もちろん、日米同盟は大事ですが、日本には日本としての考え方もあります。そこをきちんと土台にしながら、アメリカにも影響を与えていきたいと思っています。

　確かに、イスラエルの方々は、アメリカに対する影響力を増すために、非常に濃厚なロビー活動をされておられますので、そういうものを、われわれも勉強しなければいけないとは思います。
　ただ、今までのキリスト教とユダヤ教の世界観だけでは地球を覆い尽くせません。やはり、それには限界があります。

2 An Interview with the Guardian Spirit of Benjamin Netanyahu, Prime Minister of Israel

If Happy Science does not take action, wars and conflicts will never end, so we will make efforts to reconcile all religions in this world.

Netanyahu's G.S.   You should research about the Muslims. What do you think about the human bombs of the Muslims? Is it a good thing?

Tsuiki   We hope to put a stop to such things as well.

Netanyahu's G.S.   They say that they were influenced by a Japanese tradition. Is that true?

Tsuiki   I think you are referring to the kamikaze.

Netanyahu's G.S.   Kamikaze. Harakiri.

第2章　イスラエル首相・ネタニヤフ氏守護霊インタヴュー

　このまま放っておくと、今後も戦争が絶えないでしょうから、私どもとしては、しっかりと「宗教の融和」ができるようにしていきたいと考えております。

ネタニヤフ守護霊　君たちは、もっとイスラム教徒を研究したほうがいいね。イスラム教徒の"人間爆弾"については、どう思っているのかね？　それはいいことなのか？

立木　要するに、そういうものをなくしていきたいと思いますので、イスラム教にも……。

ネタニヤフ守護霊　彼らは、「日本の伝統に影響を受けた」と言っているが、それは本当か？

立木　日本の"神風"のことをおっしゃっていると思うのですが……。

ネタニヤフ守護霊　カミカゼ、ハラキリ。

Tsuiki Kamikaze is a military tactic and is only used against the military. Terrorism is done towards civilians, so I think there is a difference between human bombs and kamikaze fighters.

Netanyahu's G.S. They are under-developed people, you know? They should obey us. We are intelligent people. We have a lot of Nobelists. No?

Tsuiki Western countries have a history of imperialism and have exploited many countries, causing trouble for many countries in Asia and Africa. In that sense, I feel that there are still some reparations and atonement to be made.

I hope that Japan can bring justice and peace to each of the countries.

Netanyahu's G.S. Oh…you need cultivation. Okay?

立木　あの"神風"は、軍隊に対して行ったものです。一方、今の自爆テロは、一般市民のなかで実行していますから、これには、やはり違う部分があると思います。

ネタニヤフ守護霊　彼らは、未開の人間だ。そうだろう？ だから、彼らは、われわれに従わなければならない。われわれは、知的な人間だ。ユダヤ人にはノーベル賞受賞者がたくさんいる。違うか？

立木　ただ、欧米による帝国主義的な歴史の問題もあります。それによって、アジアやアフリカが搾取され、虐げられるような目に遭ったわけですので、ここには、やはり何らかの清算が要るのではないでしょうか。

　日本としては、それぞれの正しいところをしっかりと踏まえた上で、きちんと調停していきたいと思います。

ネタニヤフ守護霊　君たちには教養が必要だね。いいかい？

Jesus Christ was an honest man. Muhammad was a liar. Do you know that? This is the starting point of wisdom. Right?

Tsuiki I think we need to thoroughly discuss the validity of such thinking.

10 Japan's Role in the World

Ayaori I don't think everybody will agree with your way of thinking. In that sense, I hope that Muslims and Jewish people can find common ground where they can converse.

Netanyahu's G.S. Don't misunderstand us. We are the forces that will emancipate the Islamic people from the suppression inflicted on them by evil teachings. We are the emancipators; we are like Moses. Islamic people are being suppressed. You understand?

第2章　イスラエル首相・ネタニヤフ氏守護霊インタヴュー

イエス・キリストは正直な男だった。ムハンマドは嘘つきだ。そうだろう？　ここが、知恵の始まりなんだ。そうだろう？

立木　その認識についても、今後、議論していかなければいけないと思います。

10　日本が世界に対して果たすべき役割とは

綾織　あなたのような考えは、全人類が受け入れられるものではありませんので、私たちとしては、ぜひ、イスラム教とユダヤ教の双方が話し合える点を探っていきたいと思っています。

ネタニヤフ守護霊　われわれのことを誤解しないでくれよ。われわれは、イスラム教徒たちを、「悪しき教えによる抑圧」から解き放つ力なんだ。つまり、"解放者"なのだよ。モーセのようなね。イスラム教徒たちは、抑圧されているだろう？　分かるか？

Tsuiki I understand your point, but what you say is not entirely true.

Netanyahu's G.S. No, no, no. You are not being honest. You are not sincere.

Tsuiki It is true that there are certain aspects of Islam that should be changed.

Netanyahu's G.S. We are the spring of love, God's love. And we must save other people, our neighbors.

Ayaori Earlier, the guardian spirit of President Ahmadinejad…

Netanyahu's G.S. We must kill Khameini (Iran's Supreme Leader), and we must kill Ahmadinejad.

第2章　イスラエル首相・ネタニヤフ氏守護霊インタヴュー

立木　そういう面もあるでしょうが、ただ、全部がそうとも言い切れないのではないでしょうか。

ネタニヤフ守護霊　いやいや、その君の言い方は、正直でも誠実でもない。

立木　いいえ。実際に、イスラム教にも変えていくべきことはあると思います。

ネタニヤフ守護霊　われわれは、愛の泉、神の愛の泉なのだ。そして、他の人々、隣人たちを助けなければならないのだ。

綾織　先ほど、アフマディネジャド大統領の守護霊も……。

ネタニヤフ守護霊　だから、ハメネイ（イランの最高指導者）を殺さなければならないし、このアフマディネジャドも殺さなければならない。

Ayaori   The guardian spirit of President Ahmadinejad had a similar opinion about Prime Minister Netayahu.

Tsuiki   Both of you have the same opinion about each other.

Ayaori   Listening to the two of you speak today, I now understand that you will never agree nor reconcile with each other. However, we hope to help bring peace between both countries.

Tsuiki   We hope that as a country, Japan will have more power and influence in the world.

Ayaori   Thank you for taking time out of your busy schedule to come today.

Netanyahu's G.S.   Don't forget. You, Japan, and the

第２章　イスラエル首相・ネタニヤフ氏守護霊インタヴュー

綾織　アフマディネジャド大統領の守護霊も、あなたと同じようなことをおっしゃっていました。

立木　お互いさまということですね。

綾織　今までのお話から、「これはもう、お互いに平行線で、簡単には交わらない」ということが非常によく分かりました。ただ、それを何とかできるように、私たちも協力していきたいと思います。

立木　日本としても、もう少し力をつけていきたいと思います。

綾織　本日は、お忙しいなか、本当にありがとうございました。

ネタニヤフ守護霊　忘れるなよ。君たち日本とアメリカは、

United States of America have an alliance relationship. You are in a US-Japan alliance.

Ayaori Yes indeed, we are in an alliance, but Japan will have its own opinions.

Tsuiki Japan will never hold biases against Jewish people. I think that our history has proven this.

Netanyahu's G.S. Yeah, yeah. That's right. That's right. I know. I know.

Tsuiki We will make efforts so that Jewish people and Muslims can become friends.

Netanyahu's G.S. The Muslims are very poor people, you know!? They surrendered to devils!

同盟関係にある。日米同盟があるのだ。

綾織　同盟はありますが、今後、「日本としての考え方」も出てくると思います。

立木　ただ、日本は、ユダヤ人を差別したりはしません。今までの歴史もご存じだとは思いますが……。

ネタニヤフ守護霊　ああ、そうだ、そうだ。知ってるよ。知っている。

立木　ですから、今後、ユダヤ教徒とイスラム教徒とが、何とか仲良くできるように努力していきたいと考えております。

ネタニヤフ守護霊　イスラム教徒は、かなり貧しい人々だ。そうだろう？　彼らは、悪魔に屈したのだ。

Ayaori I think that it is one of Japan's roles to assist the Islamic countries and help the Muslims become prosperous.

Netanyahu's G.S. Ahh… Uh huh.

Tsuiki Thank you very much for coming today.

Okawa Okay. (To the guardian spirit of Netanyahu) Thank you very much.

11 Will the Tensions Between Iran and Israel Lead to Mankind's Final War?

Okawa It looks like there's little we can do about this. They might have to fight it out. Would this become the final war?

綾織　もちろん、「イスラム圏に対する支援を通じて、イスラム教徒の方々に豊かになってもらうことも、日本の役割である」と思っています。

ネタニヤフ守護霊　あー。ああ。

立木　今日は、本当にありがとうございました。

大川隆法　はい。(ネタニヤフ守護霊に) ありがとうございました。

11　両国の対立は最終戦争になるのか

大川隆法　ああ。これは、もう、どうしようもないですね。まあ、喧嘩をしてもらうしかないですけれども、どうなんでしょうか。これは最終戦争になるのでしょうか。

Tsuiki If nobody stops them, I think it would.

Okawa They are both extremely hard-liners; hawk against hawk. They might fight until one of them finally loses.

Israel will probably keep fighting so long as it exists. It is a horrible thing to want to annihilate the entire Arab world.

But it is true that Israel already possesses nuclear weapons. And then if it succeeds in getting the international consensus, Israel would have complete advantage.

Iran, however, believes that it has friendly relations with Japan, that Japan is not a Christian country.

Furthermore, Iran's political system has striking resemblances with the Japanese Shinto religion.

Tsuiki Yes, it does.

　　　　　　第2章　イスラエル首相・ネタニヤフ氏守護霊インタヴュー

立木　放っておいたら、そうなりかねません。

大川隆法　すごいタカ派同士であり、タカ対タカの戦いなので、どちらかが負けるまで行くのでしょうか。

　イスラエルがあり続けるかぎり、イスラエルはアラブ圏との戦いを続けるでしょうね。しかし、「アラブ圏を全滅させる」というのは大変なことです。
　ただ、そういう意味では、イスラエルのほうは核兵器を持っていますからね。これで国際合意まで取り付けたら、圧倒的に優位な立場に立つことは事実でしょう。

　一方、イランの人たちは、「日本はイランとも友好関係にある」「日本はクリスチャンの国ではない」と思っているんですよね。
　また、イランの政治体制を見ると、実は、日本神道とよく似ているところがあります。

立木　そうですね。

Okawa Iran's political system, which has been dominated by the Shiites, is also a hereditary institution that has been lasting a very long time. It is very similar to Japan's Emperial system. Happy Science staffs are over there right now holding seminars. Iran and Japan seem to share a few similarities.

What shall we do? This is a difficult issue, isn't it?

If we look only at the numbers, there are more Muslims.

Tsuiki Yes.

Okawa There are one billion Muslims, whereas there are only over ten million Jews. The outcome is clear if you judge solely based on numbers.

However, if Israel reasons that God is on their side and persuades the Christians to support it, on the grounds that Israel is their Holy Land too, then they

大川隆法 イランは、血統主義のシーア派でずっと続いており、日本の天皇制に極めて似た政治形態を取っています。今、当会はイランでセミナーをしていますが、イランには何か少し日本に似ているところがあるのです。

　どうしましょうか。困りましたね。
　数の原理で行けば、ムスリム（イスラム教徒）の数のほうが多いですからね。

立木　はい、そうです。

大川隆法　イスラム教には10億人の信者がいて、もう片方（ユダヤ教）には、千数百万人しか信者がいないので、数の原理で言えば、結論は、はっきりしています。
　しかし、イスラエルが、「神の正義は、こちらにある」という言い方をしたり、「ここはキリスト教の聖地だから」という言い方をしたりすれば、20億人のキリスト教徒を

could draw two billion people to their side. It would become a fight between one billion and two billion. That would truly spell doomsday for humankind.

Mr. Obama will do his best to placate the situation.

North Korea failed in test launching its intercontinental ballistic missiles, so the potential date of an attack from the U.S. has been pushed back. Now, the U.S. will turn its attention to Iran.

So the U.S. is restraining Israel from attacking Iran. Israel will not want to wait to make a surprise attack because the earlier they strike, the more effect it will have.

What can we do?

味方に引っ張ってこられるのです。10億人対20億人の戦いになると、本当に人類破滅の最終戦争になる可能性はありますね。

　オバマさんは一生懸命に融和政策を採ろうとするでしょう。

　今、北朝鮮は、長距離弾道ミサイルの発射に失敗したので、アメリカから攻撃を受ける機会は少し先になったかもしれません。そのため、次はイランにアメリカの関心が移るでしょうね。

　ただ、イスラエルも、今、一生懸命、攻撃を抑えていると思うんですよ。イスラエルはイランに急襲をかけたいでしょうし、早めに叩けば、それだけ効果が大きいので、やりたいところでしょう。

　うーん。困りましたねえ。

12 The Only Solution Is to Spread Happy Science Teachings

Okawa Our members in Iran have just about exceeded one hundred. I suppose that's the extent of our membership in Iran right now. I wonder how many members we have in Israel. I don't know.

But I imagine missionary work would be difficult there, too.

Tsuiki I agree.

Okawa Creating members might be close to impossible in Israel. Once you become a Happy Science member, you would cease to be a Jew.

Tsuiki That's true. You would no longer fit the definition of a Jew.

12 幸福の科学の教えを弘めるしかない

大川隆法　当会のイランの信者は百人を超えたぐらいですか。まだ、そんなところでしょうかね。

　ところで、イスラエルには、当会の信者は何人かいるのですか。私は知りませんが、ここも伝道が難しい国でしょうね。

立木　そうですね。

大川隆法　ここは信者が"獲得不能"かもしれない国です。ここでは、当会の信者になったら、ユダヤ人ではなくなるのでしょうからね。

立木　そうですね（笑）。定義的には、そうなります（注。ユダヤ人を「ユダヤ教徒」と捉える場合）。

Okawa Right. Jews cannot by definition believe in two gods.

This is a tough one. What to do, what to do. I wonder which country, Iran or Israel, Happy Science would spread in quicker…

Tsuiki Either way, it will have a great impact.

Okawa Since the Republican Party of America has relatively close ties to Jewish money, siding with the Republicans would put us on Israel's side, while our missionary activities in Islamic countries would make us look like we are rooting for the Muslims. As a result, people might see us as egging on both.

The ability of Happy Science members to persuade Jews and Christians to believe in a different God will rest on the extent of Happy Science's influence. We ourselves have to grow into a world religion.

第2章　イスラエル首相・ネタニヤフ氏守護霊インタヴュー

大川隆法　そうなんです。だからそれでは駄目なんですよね。ここでは「二神」はありえないんでしょうから。

　これは難しいですね。ああ、どうしましょうか。うーん。当会の教えが、イランとイスラエルの、どちらのほうに広がるかといえば……。

立木　その影響は大きいと思います。

大川隆法　アメリカの共和党系は、どちらかというと、ユダヤ資本のほうに近いので、共和党側につくと、イスラエル応援型になるし、イスラム圏で伝道をすると、イスラム側への応援になって、結果的には、当会が両方をけしかけるような感じになるのかもしれませんね。

　また、ユダヤ教徒やキリスト教徒が、当会の信者から、「従来の信仰を捨てて、別なものを信仰しなさい」と言われても、それで納得するとは思えません。やはり、そこには、「幸福の科学の実勢力が、どの程度まで及ぶか」と

183

Otherwise, they could easily tell us that we are the ethnic religion.

Still, Israel does not seem to have ill feelings towards Japan, nor does Iran. It gives Japan a little room to offer help.

Iran is using the same rhetoric as North Korea in justifying the development of nuclear weapons. They are saying that their nuclear energy development is for power. Iran is irritated that the world sees them as a country similar to North Korea.

Israel and Iran, no matter what, will continue to hold conflicting opinions.

Jesus seems to be taking a neutral stance. You would almost think that he's letting them believe as they will, and fight it out on their own.

Tsuiki   Yes.

第２章　イスラエル首相・ネタニヤフ氏守護霊インタヴュー

いう問題があり、こちらも世界宗教にまでなっていないと、説得力がないのです。間違いなく、「そちらこそ民族宗教だろうが」と言われるでしょう。

　ただ、イスラエルもイランも、日本に悪感情を持っているわけではないので、確かに、日本が何らかのお役に立てる可能性はあるでしょうね。

　イランも、本当は核兵器をつくりたいのでしょうが、今のところ、北朝鮮と同じような言い方で、「核エネルギーによる発電をして何が悪い」と言っているのでしょうし、北朝鮮扱いをされていることに対しては、腹に据えかねているところがあるんでしょうね。

　今の状態では、イランとイスラエルのどちらに訊いても、答えは必ず正反対になるでしょう。

　天上界のイエスは、あまり、両陣営の対立の責任を取っていませんね（会場笑）。どう見ても、そうです。勝手に喧嘩させているような感じでしょうか。

立木　そういうことですね。

Okawa The way Mr. Netanyahu's guardian spirit put it made it sound as if the Seven Archangels are fighting; as if Michael and Gabriel are warring against each other. This concerns me.

I'm sure the key to solving the problem is somewhere…

I suppose there isn't much we can do but to export our teachings and spread it.

Tsuiki Yes.

第2章　イスラエル首相・ネタニヤフ氏守護霊インタヴュー

大川隆法　ネタニヤフ守護霊の今の言い方だと、まるで、七大天使同士が戦っているようにも聞こえました。ミカエルとガブリエルが戦っているかのような言い方をしていましたが、これは非常によろしくない感じではあります。

　何か「解決のキー」があるかもしれないのですけれども……。

　まあ、しかたがありませんね。当会の教えを輸出して弘(ひろ)めるしかないでしょう。

立木　そうですね。はい。

13 Israel's Surprise Attack Could Start a War?

Okawa It would be extremely problematic if a war starts between Christians and Muslims, which would be a battle between two billion people and one billion people.

I got the impression that Iran wants Japan to intercede. To them, Japan is the only country that can persuade the US. But, I'm afraid that Japan is not strong enough.

Tsuiki Yes. Japan right now does not have that kind of power.

Okawa Iran believes that a ten percent discount on oil will be enough to encourage Japan to talk to the United States.

This really is a difficult issue because we don't have

13 戦争はイスラエルの奇襲で始まる？

大川隆法　ただ、キリスト教とイスラム教に、「20億対10億の戦い」をされるのは、けっこうきついですね。

　イランのほうは、「日本に仲介してほしい」という思いを持っているのではないかと感じられます。「アメリカを説得できるのは日本しかない」と思っているようですが、日本が弱いので、ちょっと……。

立木　そうですね。日本には、まだ、そこまでの力はありません。

大川隆法　イランは、「日本向けの原油を、10パーセント、ディスカウントする」と言い、その程度で日本が何かをしてくれると思っているかもしれません。
　いや、なかなか難しいですね。まあ、こちらにも、イ

a deep understanding of their cultures, both Iran and Israel.

If we had put the two state heads against each other in a debate, it would have turned into a fist fight.

Tsuiki　Yes.

Okawa　Shall we end it here then?

Their claims were as we predicted anyways.

This conflict originates in their differing concepts of God passed down by their respective religious leaders.

Actually, Judaism and Christianity also have differences and have a history of conflicts. Here, Israel is contradicting itself.

What can I say? All we can do is to try to bring them together.

Yet, to convince them, we need more power, both

第2章　イスラエル首相・ネタニヤフ氏守護霊インタヴュー

ランやイスラエルのことを、文明として十分に理解できていないところがあるんですけどね。

　これでは、この二人でディベートをしても、つかみ合いになるだけでしょう。駄目ですね。

立木　はい。

大川隆法　もう、このへんでやめましょうか。

　両者とも、予想どおりの言い分を言っているだけでしたね。

　もともとは、「神の概念」のところから見解が分かれ、それぞれ、歴代の宗教指導者たちが、ずっと教え続けてきたものでしょう。

　本当のことを言えば、「ユダヤ教とキリスト教だって違う」ということで、"戦争"をしたこともあるはずなので、ここの矛盾はあるわけです。

　まあ、しかたがないですね。いちおう融合するしかないのでしょうか。

　当会は、政治的にも、宗教的にも、もう一段の力を持

as a religion and as a political party.

Tsuiki   Yes, I agree.

Okawa   The guardian spirit of Netanyahu pointed out that our members are fewer than the number of Jews. We need to work a little harder.

He also said that the Jewish religion has produced a lot of Nobel Laureates.

Tsuiki   Yes he did.

Okawa   As for Muslims, their readiness to take human life is sometimes appalling and gives the impression that they have little regard for human life. They should consider changing this way of thinking.

Since Islam became established as a religion through wars, you can see that they had this way of thinking from the beginning, which can rationalize their use

たないと、彼らに対して説得力が出ないようです。

立木　そうですね。はい。

大川隆法　「ユダヤ教徒より信者が少ないのではないか」と言われているようなので、もう少し頑張らないといけないですね。
　ネタニヤフ守護霊は、「ユダヤ人にはノーベル賞受賞者がたくさんいる」とも言っていました。

立木　そうですね。

大川隆法　イスラム系には、凄惨なところというか、殺すのが早いというか、人の命を少し軽く感じている面があることはあるので、このへんについては、多少、考えを改めさせなくてはいけないと思います。
　イスラム教は戦争に勝って立ち上がった宗教なので、その立ち上げ方から見れば、今の“人間爆弾”、自爆テロについても、そういう面はあったようにも感じられます。

of human bombs, the suicide bombers. However, the problem is that this way of fighting is no longer effective against modern weapons.

That is why they think that taking measures to modernize their countries is "good." Otherwise they would become slaves to Israel. Modernization is a must if they wish to avert such an end.

It is a difficult issue but let's do what we can.

Tsuiki　Yes.

Okawa　However, today's spiritual messages could be a turning point. It may sound like a Zen riddle, but by teaching them,"God's teachings can be expressed differently depending on the times in which it was taught. So, God was guiding people back then a certain way, but he actually wanted to teach

ただ、「その戦い方が近代兵器に通用しなくなっている」というところが問題なのでしょう。

　だから、近代化を進めていくことを、彼らは「善だ」と思っているわけです。「今のままだったら、イスラエルの奴隷になってしまう」ということでしょう？　その危機を回避するために、近代化を進めているんでしょうからね。
　難しいですが、当会としては、やるべきことをやりましょうか。

立木　はい。

大川隆法　でも、今日の霊言収録は一つの契機ではあるので、禅問答のようかもしれませんが、私たちが、彼らに、「いや、神の考えは時代によって違うのだ。その時代には、そのように指導しただけで、本当は、こういう考えなのだ」ということを教えることによって、それが何らかの話し合いの材料になるといいんですけどね。

about 'this'." I hope this could serve as a basis for conversation.

Hmm...Would this clash turn into a final war? Not to mention, a war would start with Israel's surprise attack. They would first start by destroying the nuclear power plants.

All they need for that is to obtain long-distance refueling aircrafts and a hundred or so combat aircrafts, so it is very possible that it will happen.

The question is whether we can convince them otherwise.

In addition, there is a high possibility that Iran and North Korea have secret ties. Iran could also be secretly negotiating with China, since China is expanding its influence into Iran.

Indeed, it is a difficult issue.

第2章　イスラエル首相・ネタニヤフ氏守護霊インタヴュー

　うーん。最終戦争になるでしょうか。あるいは、イスラエル側の奇襲攻撃で始まるのが普通でしょうか。その場合は、おそらく、イランの原子力プラントを叩き潰すところから始まるでしょうね。
　イスラエルが長距離の給油機を手に入れて、百機ほどの攻撃機で攻撃できれば、イランを叩けるのでしょうから、やはり、現実性としては高いと思われます。
　本気で、これを説得できるでしょうか。

　さらに、イランは、確かに、北朝鮮とも地下でつながっている可能性があります。中国ともつながっているかもしれません。中国も、こちらのほうに手を伸ばしてきていますからね。
　うーん。なかなか難しいですね。

14 Happy Science Must Increase Its Influence and Gain a Higher Perspective

Okawa   In addition to increasing our influence, we need to gain a higher perspective. Both Happy Science and the Happiness Realization Party might need to get their names known more widely.

Tsuiki   We will work on that.

Okawa   It doesn't seem like they'll listen to your mediation anytime soon.

Tsuiki   I will do my best.

Okawa   You got him mad. He said, "I'm the President!" Even the Japanese media can rarely get to

14　勢力を広げつつ、見識を高める努力を

大川隆法　だから、当会は、勢力を広げつつ、見識を高めなくてはいけないんですね。やはり、ハッピー・サイエンスや、ハピネス・リアライゼーション・パーティー（幸福実現党）には、もう少し知名度が要りますね。

立木　はい。かしこまりました。

大川隆法　「立木党首の仲裁」ということでは、イランもイスラエルも、なかなか聴いてくれそうにありませんからね（笑）。

立木　これから頑張ってまいります。はい。

大川隆法　アフマディネジャド氏の守護霊は、「私は大統領だぞ」と言って怒っていましたが、日本のマスコミも、

interview him.

But it was better than doing nothing. It also provided information for developing an opinion. I would be glad if Happy Science could contribute something for resolving this issue.

Unexpectedly, we might be able to penetrate the Islamic countries by spreading our teachings and increasing our members in Africa.

We do not speak ill of Jesus Christ or of the ancient Jewish prophets. In fact, we embrace them, so we are not like the nationalistic Shinto religion that gripped Japan during World War II.

So I hope we can bring Islam and Judaism together.

If Happy Science becomes famous in Africa, we might have a chance at approaching the Middle East from the African continent, since they are close to each other, and also from India.

第2章　イスラエル首相・ネタニヤフ氏守護霊インタヴュー

アフマディネジャド大統領本人には、なかなか取材できないでしょうね。

　まあ、何もしないよりはましでしょうし、少しは見解を出せるでしょう。「当会がお役に立てれば、ありがたい」と思います。

　意外に、アフリカで伝道をして当会の教えを広げ、アフリカの信者が増えていくと、イスラム圏のほうに教えが入っていくこともあるでしょう。

　また、当会は、イエスや古代ユダヤの預言者等を悪く言っているわけではなく、きちんと受け入れているので、先の大戦における国家神道とは違うと思います。ああいうかたちではないです。

　だから、当会が中東をうまくまとめられるとよろしいですね。

　でも、アフリカと中東は近いですからね。当会がアフリカでそうとう有名になってきたら、アフリカとインドの両方から、中東に当会の教えが入っていくこともあるかもしれませんね。

Japan's economic recovery also has a vital role in resolving this issue in the Middle East. Japan's economy must go up another notch in strength.

Tsuiki　Absolutely.

Okawa　Japan can't afford to sink. This is something we need to work very hard on.

Tsuiki　Right. We'll do all we can.

Okawa　We're still left with a lot of issues to tackle but let's call it a day. Thank you.

それと、日本の経済的復活も関係はあるでしょう。もう一段、日本経済の力が強くならなくてはいけません。

立木　そうですね。はい。

大川隆法　日本が沈んだら駄目ですね。そのあたりを、うまくやらなくてはいけないでしょう。

立木　しっかりと、それに取り組んでまいります。

大川隆法　課題は残りましたが、以上にしましょう。お疲れさまでした。

イラン大統領 vs. イスラエル首相
――中東の核戦争は回避できるのか――

2012年5月17日　初版第1刷

著　者　　大　川　隆　法

発　行　　幸福実現党
　　　　　〒107-0052　東京都港区赤坂2丁目10番8号
　　　　　TEL(03)6441-0754

発　売　　幸福の科学出版株式会社
　　　　　〒107-0052　東京都港区赤坂2丁目10番14号
　　　　　TEL(03)5573-7700
　　　　　http://www.irhpress.co.jp/

印刷・製本　　株式会社 堀内印刷所

落丁・乱丁本はおとりかえいたします
©Ryuho Okawa 2012. Printed in Japan. 検印省略
ISBN978-4-86395-199-0 C0030
Photo: AP/アフロ、ロイター/アフロ

幸福実現党
THE HAPPINESS REALIZATION PARTY

党員大募集!

あなたも 幸福実現党 の党員になりませんか。

未来を創る「幸福実現党」を支え、ともに行動する仲間になろう!

党員になると

○幸福実現党の理念と綱領、政策に賛同する18歳以上の方なら、どなたでもなることができます。党費は、一人年間5,000円です。
○資格期間は、党費を入金された日から1年間です。
○党員には、幸福実現党の機関紙が送付されます。

申し込み書は、下記、幸福実現党公式サイトでダウンロードできます。

幸福実現党 本部　〒107-0052 東京都港区赤坂 2-10-8　TEL03-6441-0754　FAX03-6441-0764

幸福実現党のメールマガジン "HRPニュースファイル" や "Happiness Letter" の登録ができます。

動画で見る幸福実現――幸福実現TVの紹介、党役員のブログの紹介も!

幸福実現党の最新情報や、政策が詳しくわかります!

幸福実現党公式サイト

http://www.hr-party.jp/

もしくは 幸福実現党 検索

大川隆法ベストセラーズ・あらゆる宗教の壁を越えて

不滅の法
宇宙時代への目覚め

「霊界」、「奇跡」、「宇宙人」の存在。物質文明が封じ込めてきた不滅の真実が、いま、解き放たれようとしている。地球の未来を切り拓くために。

2,000円

救世の法
信仰と未来社会

信仰を持つことの功徳や、民族・宗教対立を終わらせる考え方など、人類への希望が示される。地球神の説くほんとうの「救い」とは──。

1,800円

世界紛争の真実
ミカエル vs. ムハンマド

キリスト教を援護するミカエルと、イスラム教開祖ムハンマドの霊言が、両文明衝突の真相を明かす。宗教の対立を乗り越えるための必読の書。

1,400円

発売　幸福の科学出版株式会社　　　※表示価格は本体価格（税別）です。

大川隆法ベストセラーズ・日本と世界の平和を考える

平和への決断
国防なくして繁栄なし

軍備拡張を続ける中国。財政赤字に苦しみ、アジアから引いていくアメリカ。世界の潮流が変わる今、日本人が「決断」すべきこととは。
【幸福実現党刊】

1,500円

日本武尊の国防原論
緊迫するアジア有事に備えよ

アメリカの衰退、日本を狙う中国、北朝鮮の核──。緊迫するアジア情勢に対し、日本武尊が、日本を守り抜く「必勝戦略」を語る。
【幸福実現党刊】

1,400円

ロシア・プーチン 新大統領と帝国の未来
守護霊インタヴュー

中国が覇権主義を拡大させるなか、ロシアはどんな国家戦略をとるのか!? また、親日家プーチン氏の意外な過去世も明らかに。
【幸福実現党刊】

1,300円

発売　幸福の科学出版株式会社　　　　※表示価格は本体価格（税別）です。